12
CHARACTERISTICS
OF A
Godly
WOMAN

A 12-WEEK JOURNEY OF DEVELOPING
THE GODLY WOMAN WITHIN YOU

BIBLE STUDY

12 CHARACTERISTICS of a GODLY WOMAN

A 12-Week Journey of Developing the Godly Woman Within You
BIBLE STUDY 2019 Created and Designed by Tamara Doss

Contributing Authors: Lori Bryant, Dr. Roseanna Roman, Cathy Greer, Blanca Cisneros, Esther Rose Neal, Colleen Myers, Heather Flores, Peggy Stapleton, Nicole Forbes, Pam Booher, Cathy Guerrero, and Tamara Doss

Amazing Life Ministries
www.GodsAmazingPlans.com
Copyright© 2022 by Tamara Doss and Amazing Life Ministries

All rights reserved. No part of this publication may be reproduced, distributed, or transmitted in any form or by any means, including photocopying, recording, or other electronic or mechanical methods, without the prior written permission of the author and publisher.

Scriptures taken from The Holy Bible, New International Version™, NIV Copyright© 11975, 1978, 1984, 2011 by Biblica, Inc. Used by permission. All rights reserved worldwide.

Scriptures are taken from Amplified Bible™, Copyright© 1954, 1958, 1962, 1964, 1965, 1987 by The Lockman Foundation. Used by permission. All rights reserved.

Scriptures are taken from The Holy Bible, New Living Translation™, Copyright© 1996, 2004, 2007, and 2013 by Tyndale House Foundation. Used by permission of Tyndale House Publishers, Inc., Carol Stream, Illinois 60188. All rights reserved.

Scriptures taken from The Holy Bible, New King James Version™, Copyright© 1982 by Thomas Nelson, Inc. Used by permission. All rights reserved.

ISBN 978-1-7325050-2-5
Published by **Amazing Life Ministries Publishing**
Printed in the United States of America

Dedication

Thank you, Father, for entrusting me with this journey and allowing me to share it with the world. Thank you for your unconditional love and guidance throughout my life. Thank you for making me beautiful and perfect in your image. Thank you for giving me the strength, courage, and boldness to be obedient to your will.

I want to dedicate this book to all my family and friends who support and love me unconditionally and believe in me, my purpose, and my relationship with God.

I dedicate this book to you; the reader and I thank you for choosing to join me and my friends on this journey and Bible Study that will change your life by spending time in the presence of Jesus daily and learning from other women who are on the journey of developing God's character daily and become the Godly women He designed us to be.

I know there are many struggles, questions, and obstacles that have prevented you from courageously living free and I pray this journey will transform your heart, mind, and soul. Jesus is waiting for you, and I am confident that if you seek Him, you will find Him, and He will develop the Godly woman within you. He has already created her, and His character is planted in you. Discover Him and you will discover yourself.

I dedicate this book to God my Father, Jesus my best friend and Holy Spirit, my guide to living life on Earth as it is in Heaven.

Acknowledgments

I want to thank my wonderful husband, Reggie, for your unconditional love and support. Thank you for never allowing me to give up on who I am and what God has called me to do. Thank you for your confidence and belief in me and my relationship with Jesus Christ. Your faith in my relationship with God and belief in me drove me to continue this journey and I love you with all my heart. I am blessed by your unconditional love and support.

To my three amazing children Ricci, Robbi, and Ronni. Thank you for being you and I am so blessed to have you in my life. I am grateful that God entrusted me to be your mommy. God has great favor on your lives, and He has an amazing plan for each of you. I pray each of you discovers it and bravely lives it out in full color.

To my mother, father, brothers, and friends, thank you for believing in me and supporting me in my many life endeavors. Your love and belief in me mean so much to me and I could not be who I am without your love and support throughout the years.

To my many mentors, some know who you are, and some do not, thank you for all your wisdom, knowledge, and teachings that you have given me over our years of knowing one another.

To my friends, encouragers, and believers in this project, I am so grateful for your love and enthusiasm for what God has created and for sharing your firsthand experiences with the world.

I give many thanks to my awesome team of servants who made this possible through prayer, preparation, and execution of our one-day Author's Retreat. These amazing women behind the book are Denise Valdez, Marlene Weyhgandt, Pattie Castillo, and Sandy Cushing who worked tirelessly in prayer, soaking, planning, and preparing for every detail to bless the Authors and create an environment that was spiritual, loving, peaceful, and magical for writing God's words from His mouth to their ears and from their minds to their fingers and to your eyes and ears as you read their words and hear God's voice through their writing.

I am grateful for all the wonderful Authors who are friends and mentors that participated and contributed to this study.

Thank you for sharing your wisdom and individual experiences of growing and developing your Godly characteristic into the beautiful, amazing woman of God you are today. I love you and am grateful that God has placed you in my life for such a time as this. Thank you for blessing me and blessing others.

I want to thank God for giving me the guidance, strength, and focus to finish this book. It was only by the power of the Holy Spirit that this book was given and is written. Now, I surrender this assignment back to you and wait patiently to see your will be done.

12

CHARACTERISTICS
OF A
Godly

WOMAN

A 12-WEEK JOURNEY OF DEVELOPING
THE GODLY WOMAN WITHIN YOU

BIBLE STUDY

Welcome from Tamara Doss

I am so excited that you decided to join me and my friends on this 12-week BIBLE STUDY created from an incredible vision the Lord had given me on an early Saturday morning in December 2018 on my way to a local women's conference.

The Lord spoke to me as I was driving and asked me to author a book called "12 Characteristics of a Godly Woman". I responded to Him in a whisper, "That is a great title, Lord." He then proceeded to tell me, "I want you to teach women about these characteristics and to help them recognize they can develop and walk in not just one or two of them but grow in all twelve characteristics just like my Son Jesus."

He then listed out all twelve characteristics for me and I got excited because He was showing me what each character's value was and how women have been deceived by the enemy that they do not possess these Godly characteristics or carry the value of them confidently. He wanted to restore the truth to them through this teaching and walk hand in hand with them to reflect His character in their lives.

I thought His ideas were wonderful and then He blew me away. He told me, "Pray over each characteristic I have revealed to you, and then think of the women in your life that have displayed each characteristic and ask them to write a chapter in this book." Amazing! And so, I did.

And if that was not enough, He started listing the names of the eleven amazing women with the Godly characteristic He had spoken into existence. He would not let this go! He was so persistent and kept saying for the next three days, "Call them, call them, call them." And so, I did.

Six months later and after much prayer, planning, and more prayer, we launched a one-day Author Retreat on June 3, 2019, in my California home and we drafted this book in one day. We have interviews, Author insights on their Godly characteristic, and photos of God's work for you to enjoy and step into the divine creation of this study.

**For more retreat photos,
meet the authors and author interviews
go to www.GodsAmazingPlans.com**

ENDORSEMENTS

This Bible Study will be a blessing to so many because of these amazing women of GOD. I love how each one is so different and from their past experiences, God brought this book to life and used their stories as His stories. Each woman has amazing gifts and lessons for women around the world. I related to so many of the testimonies and cried remembering what I had been through and knowing I am not the only one. I praise God! And I know God will use the foolish things of this world to confound the wise. I highly recommend this study for Women's Ministries to grow their women and enrich their lives.

        Pastor Denise Ponce, Co-Founder, Women's Leader, United in Him Christian Fellowship
        Pomona, CA

In our spinning, world–drunk culture, "12 Characteristics of a Godly Woman" is a great encouragement to every Christ-following woman in the work of Philippians 2:12, the working out of our salvation that we already obtain. Each author shares rich wisdom from their working out of lived experiences coupled with Christ. The desire and highest call to Godly character are found within these pages. Grab a few girlfriends, crack open this book and see how God will grace you in His way together.

        Laura Sonksen, Co-Founder, Pastor wife,
        South Hills Church
        Corona, CA

We all love a well-told story, and when it is based on truth; all the better. Well, this book has 12 of them! Everyone is unique and impactful. Each is threaded with the author's Holy Spirit-forged insight that stirs the reader to ponder her Godly character development. The woman who reads this book will see something of herself in these precious, personal testimonies. She may be affirmed, convicted, encouraged, refined, prompted, or challenged, but will be moved before reaching the last page of this excellent study.

        Brenda Gleason, Corona Friends Church Staff
        Corona, CA

ENDORSEMENTS

"12 Characteristics of a Godly Woman" Bible Study is a valuable asset to growing one's character and faith in Christ. It is steeped in scripture and encourages practical steps to lead a Holy life. It shares personal journeys of women's lives to follow God and teaches you to surrender in obedience and so much more. I highly recommend it for women of any age to grow their Godly character.

> **Rosalie Hamman** Elder, Rose Drive Friend Church, Director of Leadership & Curriculum Development, Equipping Leader Ministries, Co-Founder of Corona Friends Church
> Yorba Linda, CA

There are so many beautiful and majestic threads woven through each of these individually written chapters. Each thread tells the story of how God has used all things to work together, Romans 8:28. Each thread calls you to sit at the feet of Jesus first and foremost. To discover your focus, rely on God, and remember He is always, always with you. Be encouraged dear ones, God will take your everyday life experiences and use them for His glory just as He has with each of these amazing women. I encourage you to get into His Word through this study and let Him weave together the beautiful threads of your life, it will be time well spent.

> **Shelia Romanski,** Founder of Crystal Rose
> Holiday Island, AR

Wow, wow, wow!!!! I love how real women of God share their love for Jesus and teach how to authentically live out your life running after the heart of God in this book! If you are looking for practical ways to apply the Characteristics of Christ to your life, this is the book to read! I was so moved by the authors' transparency and ways to practically apply the principles of God to your life! A must-read!!!!

> **Natalie Morales,** Pastor, Founder of Courageous Woman Ministries
> Fontana, CA

ENDORSEMENTS

As women we have many demands screaming for our attention and management and in the process of juggling life, we can lose the meaning and purpose of what we were created to become, a woman of Godly character. This Bible Study will provide you with a Biblical perspective and the practical life equipping knowledge and skills needed to develop these Godly characteristics as you pursue your goals and look to become the best version of yourself.

>**Lawanda Martinez,** Creative Consultant, Author, Speaker, Small Group Leader, and Intercessor
>Rancho Cucamonga, CA

We are so excited about the new book from our good friend Tamara Doss and know you will be blessed abundantly and grow in God's image and Godly character when you read and study along. This Bible Study is really going to allow you to see our Heavenly Father and our Lord and Savior Jesus Christ in a brighter and glorious way. We highly encourage you to gather your friends and study together as this book will change your lives and character. Psalms 127

>**Pastor Frank and First Lady Cassandra Starks**
>In Him Global Media, KCWG Radio
>Lindale, TX

Tamara Doss did an amazing job bringing 11 other women of God together to write a book on key topics and concerns of everyone. The women are from different backgrounds, denominations, and places in life but their love and trust in God come out through the pages of each chapter. The writers are open about their personal lives, struggles and victories as they trust and lean on God. This is a unique book written by 12 women who all love the Lord and want others to know and love Him as well.

>**Pastor Tom & Carol Lance**
>Pastor Emeritus, Small Groups Pastor,
>The Grove Church
>Riverside, CA

TABLE OF CONTENTS

                                                                       PAGE

Chapter 1
GODLY CHARACTERISTIC #1 ---------------------------- 15
SEEK GOOD FIRST By Tamara Doss

Chapter 2
GODLY CHARACTERISTIC #2 ---------------------------- 37
LOVE UNCONDITIONALLY By Lori Bryant

Chapter 3
GODLY CHARACTERISTIC #3 ---------------------------- 51
PRAYERFUL LIFE By Ester Rose Neal

Chapter 4
GODLY CHARACTERISTIC #4 ---------------------------- 67
OBEDIENCE By Cathy Greer

Chapter 5
GODLY CHARACTERISTIC #5 ---------------------------- 85
FAMILY FIRST By Blanca Cisneros

Chapter 6
GODLY CHARACTERISTIC #6 ---------------------------- 105
HUMILITY By Pam Booher

Chapter 7
GODLY CHARACTERISTIC #7 ---------------------------- 119
SERVANT HEART By Nicole Forbes

TABLE OF CONTENTS

PAGE

Chapter 8
GODLY CHARACTERISTIC #8 ---------------------------- 135
HONOR & RESPECT by Dr. Roseanna Roman

Chapter 9
GODLY CHARACTERISTIC #9 ---------------------------- 147
FAITHFULNESS By Peggy Stapleton

Chapter 10
GODLY CHARACTERISTIC #10 ---------------------------163
FRUIT OF THE SPIRIT By Colleen Myers

Chapter 11
GODLY CHARACTERISTIC #11 -------------------------- 181
HOSPITALITY By Heather Flores

Chapter 12
GODLY CHARACTERISTIC #12 -------------------------- 197
STEWARDSHIP WISDOM By Dr. Cathy Guerrero

SPECIAL CONTENT

CELEBRATION AND TESTIMONY WRITING   217

LEADERS GUIDE   218

SPECIAL DEDICATION   233

LEADER TIPS
FOR LEADING THIS STUDY

-Create a comfortable, welcoming, warm, loving environment and share your heart with the women of your intent, desire, and hope for this Bible study.

-Each week assign a chapter reading and homework to study on their own or you can read the chapter together in study and then answer group discussion questions. Use whichever is best for your group of women.

-If you read the chapter in class, assign the homework for the week on their own until next week's study.

-Break into smaller groups to encourage more discussion for the group questions. Depending on the time available, you may only be able to pick several questions to focus on for discussion.

-Each week, after prayer and worship, begin the study by reviewing last week's homework briefly and then proceed to a new chapter. Ask them about important revelations they received from God and share them.

-Read the Author's prayer for the week's characteristic and then focus on having each woman write their prayer for themselves to help develop the Godly characteristic they are learning. Have them read and pray over it daily. Encourage them to ask God for help in developing His character in them.

-Pray over your group of women and bless their week of study until you meet again. Pray for them often through the week.

Godly Characteristic #1
Seek God First

But seek first His Kingdom and His righteousness, and all these things will be given to you as well.

Matthew 6:33

Tamara Doss

The Grove Church,
Riverside CA
Amazing Life Ministries
God's Amazing Plans Radio
Show, Author, and Speaker

Tamara Doss is married to Reggie Doss and mother of three funny, gifted, and precious adopted boys Ricci, Robbi, and Ronni living in Riverside, CA. She has attended Corona Friends Church for 24 years and five years ago they started to attend Grove Community Church in Riverside. Reggie and she led Holy Matrimony Marriage Ministry, as well as Tamara, who led Extraordinary Women Ministry. In 2016, she founded Amazing Life Ministries with the mission of encouraging men and women, young and old, to boldly live out God's amazing plans.

Tamara has 35 years of experience in marketing and business management. She is innovative, progressive, and desires to see people achieve their best and break new ground in their professional and personal lives so they can confidently live out God's amazing plans with the abundant life Jesus promises.

Tamara is an author, speaker, and blogger. She is a featured writer in global Christian magazines and a published author of multiple books. Tamara has been the keynote speaker at ministry and community conferences, local city prayer breakfasts, and many local charities and organizations. Tamara has been recognized by the National Association of Women Business Owners honoree of Amazing Women of the Inland Empire, Featured on KCWG Radio, Hope Radio, HSBN.TV and Radio Host of God's Amazing Plans. You can contact Tamara at www.GodsAmazingPlans.com, call/text 951-202-3567 or email her for more information at tamara.doss@rocketmail.com

Seek God First

Matthew 6:33 *"But seek first His Kingdom and His righteousness, and these things will be given to you as well."* I pray you will meditate on this chapter's memory verse this week and receive God's gifts of knowledge and provision.

Let us begin by learning the definitions of three words; Seek, God, and First. Then combine them all for a comprehensive understanding of these three simple words and how powerful the words, and actions, really are for our journey as we live our lives glorifying God with His character reflected in us.

SEEK is a verb making it an "action" word. Its meaning is "to act or activate something." SEEK, take action, and activate your relationship with your Heavenly Father, confidently knowing what you will find when you meet Him. To seek something is to earnestly look for it with the expectation of finding it. Unfortunately, some people often do not seek God first, instead, they seek everything else before they seek God. Here are two acronyms that remind me why I seek my Father and His heart. Use them as reminders for yourself.

SEEK= Supernatural Encouragement and Enjoyment with the King.
SEEK= Significant and Extraordinary Encounters into the Kingdom.

The definition of "seek" in the Webster dictionary is to attempt to find something. That something is God's heart and love for us. When we discover His love for us, it is easier for us to love ourselves and love others; His second commandment. And when we genuinely love others, we can learn to serve others well, just as Jesus served people. Seek also means to desire or obtain or achieve something; ask something from someone and search for someone or something. Seek also means go to a place; that place is the *secret place* with Jesus. Synonyms for seek are look for, pursue, search for, hunt, go in search of, request, invite, ask for, petition, plead for, solicit, beg for, attempt, aim, strive, endeavor, and aspire to.

The definition of "God" is the Creator and Ruler of the universe and source of all moral authority, the Supreme Being. Of course, we know God as Creator of the Heavens and Earth, love, holiness, and righteousness; God is a protective Father, who loves and nurtures His children; God is the Creator of all things; God is not a man, God is Spirit and Truth; God is the Truth that sets us free; God is powerful, He is a just Judge; He is three divine persons; Father, Son, and Holy Spirit. He is holy, loving, and perfect. God is trustworthy and safe. He alone is our salvation. Synonyms are Jehovah, the Almighty, the Supreme Being, the Deity, supreme, and adored, admired, or influential person.

"First" means coming before all others in time and order, earliest, fundamental, beginning, or initial. It means never previously done. You initialize, initiate, open with, begin and then go out. It also means in position, rank, or importance. Synonyms are highest, greatest, and foremost. Leading person and/or position.

When you combine the definitions of *seek, God, and first* you will get the most important and powerful directive to pursue the Creator of the Heavens and Earth; you initiate your day with the source of all moral authority as a leading person; you open your day with Spirit and Truth foremost because He is greatest; diligently going in search of your nurturer in order, God earliest, before all other things. You petition and pursue Him; you search for Him and invite Him to spend time with you. You aspire to and aim to make Him first priority. These are reasons we will talk about scheduling God time in your calendar and its representation of priority in your life. My prayer for you today is that you will begin to seek Jesus first, go to the secret place with Him, and find truth, power, strength, stability, understanding, knowledge, and wisdom to live your life in fullness reflecting God's character.

It was a Thursday afternoon in July 2001 when I got a phone call from my husband of sixteen years who told me he wanted a divorce. He had left weeks before this day to his home state to attend a family reunion. The night before he left, we argued and in our hurt and stubbornness, neither of us called the other one for days to check on each other. He left early that morning before I would wake and would not return to our home and marriage until months later when he came to collect his things in a U-Haul truck. When I first heard him say, "I want a divorce", my first reaction was disbelief and denial. I was immediately overcome by human emotions of insecurity, fear, inadequacy, and worry. Thoughts raced through my mind, "How will I survive?", "That I was not good enough"; all the crazy "not enoughs" and lies the enemy would try to deceive me with as He attempted to distract me so he could destroy me. BUT GOD had other plans for my life! And ladies, He has plans for your life too!

As I dropped to my knees in full surrender and found myself crying out to Him, I sought Him with my whole heart. God showed up! The Lord comforted me, and HE spoke directly to me. He said, "You are beautiful! You are good! You are perfect! You are loved and I am with you. I will never leave you." My husband had abandoned me, and walked away from our marriage, but my Father was with me, and He promised me He would not leave me.

God began to remind me who I was and said to me, "You are perfect but living in a fallen world." He reminded me, "If you remain in Me, I will remain in you," and with those words, I knew I was going to be ok. I heard His Spirit speak, *"Remain in me, as I also remain in you. No branch can bear fruit by itself; it must remain in the vine. Neither can you bear fruit unless you remain in Me."* John 15:4. I knew at that moment He would be my source of life during this season, and I would have to remain in His presence and counsel just like a branch that thrives and grows beautiful fruit. If I broke off or separated from Him, I would wither, and my spirit would die. He would be my everything as I chose to remain close to Him and not separate myself from His love for me! In that instant, I was keenly aware of and recognized a simple fact; He could not help me if I did not seek Him for the help I needed. I sought Him with all my heart. I found Him. And he loved me through my pain. He began a new work in me as we spent so much time together over the next two years and He mended my broken heart and restored me.

These moments would change my life forever and I would never look back at what I was not or could not achieve, or the lie that I was not created with a great purpose and loved by God, but instead, I walked forward in the truth God spoke *into* me that day. He said, *"With Me, all things are possible"* Matthew 19:26. He told me, "I am crazy in love with you even at this moment." Even in my brokenness, He reminded me, "I have great plans for your life and together we would begin a new journey, rebuild and I will remain by your side." This pivotal time in my life and the choice I made to draw upon God's presence that day, had come from prior conversations I had with Him. He had been teaching me through intimate encounters in preparation for difficult times and I had followed Jesus' example. I knew He was my most important source to seek for my comfort and reliance in this season.

We learn from Jesus' own life that He had an incredible relationship with His Father and sought Him daily. He would allow His Father to direct His steps and lead Him throughout each day, through challenges and desperate times like in the Garden of Gethsemane and for everyday living before He spent time with His disciples and followers. My prayer for this chapter, and even for authoring this book, is that God will speak to you about the most important decisions and actions of seeking Him first in your life; not just for hardships and desperate moments, but for everyday living; for every decision, every choice and every reaction and response you choose.

Our memory verse for this Godly characteristic is found in Matthew 6:33, *"But first seek His Kingdom and His righteousness, all these things will be given to you as well."* The next verse says, *"therefore, do not worry about tomorrow, for tomorrow will worry about itself. Each day has enough trouble of its own."* This is one of the key verses in Jesus' teaching. The context of "these things" are the basic needs of our life like food and clothing. Jesus has commanded us not to live in worry or fear about how we will obtain these things, even if we do not know where the next meal is coming from. He wants us to trust in His Heavenly Father to provide for our every need because we are valued so highly. (Matthew 6:25-32) Instead of living in constant and fruitless worry, Jesus gives His followers a different outlet for their energy: pursue God's Kingdom, trust His righteousness, and leave it to Him to take care of you and all your basic needs, *He* is your provider.

Pursuing righteousness means you become a "work in progress." It is a process and journey, not a destination. It is perfected over time through your obedience to Him, and it slowly reveals itself as evidence of your faith. You work at it every day to see its true perfection when you meet your Creator in Heaven. The word "seek" in Matthew 6:33 is a present imperative verb that means one is to pursue something and keep on pursuing it without stopping, like a work in progress, continually perfecting it. I encourage you to seek first God, His righteousness, and His Kingdom so you can receive all that God has to offer when you depend on Him for everything. I had to depend on Him for *everything, every day* in that season, and I can confidently tell you, as daughters of the King, you too can depend on Him for everything. I encourage you to pursue Him without stopping and seek Him for everything; the important, the somewhat important, and even the not-so-important details of your life.

It doesn't mean you won't have trouble, because we know that Jesus told us in John 16:33, *"I have told you these things, so that in Me you may have peace. In this world you will have trouble. But take heart! I have overcome the world."*, it does mean, however, that you will be ok. God is victorious and our earthly perspectives can regain clarity of Kingdom perspective and therefore remain hopeful and secure in His truth.

That late afternoon in July when my marriage crumbled into a thousand little pieces, my head spun, my heart broke and I was confused and desperate, I was uncertain of my future or how I would survive. I could have worried, but instead, I chose to surrender to my Father and trust Him in that hour. I did not ask for things I needed, but I sought His comfort and wisdom for immediate survival, I sought Him for His will. We have a Father that promised us that He will take care of us. I encourage you to seek Him daily, and you will find Him to be faithful.

As my grieving and healing process began, the enemy would try to destroy me with guilt and shame of the divorce, BUT GOD would fight for me when I could not fight for myself. God had an amazing plan for my life, and He was going to protect me and destroy the enemy's plan to harm me. My Father, who loved me dearly, was already working out all things together for my good. I had to remain still in His presence and learn to trust Him. Did I know I was pursuing

God's righteousness or seeking His Kingdom? To be honest, not really, I was trying to survive my circumstances. I was clinging to the little hope I had at that moment. It would be a lesson I would learn later when the realization came, *I made it*! Then, and only then, did I learn how much He comforted me through the journey of seeking Him for everything I needed to survive, and eventually thrive. You see, I was just a new "Christian". Only several years prior did I truly surrender my heart to Jesus and started serving God by teaching first and second-grade Sunday School. I was just beginning my journey of faith and thank God I had!

I remember after that phone call and those heartbreaking words from my husband, the loneliness and self-worthlessness I felt. I felt like I had failed, and the shame attached to that failure felt as deep as the ocean. It was not going to dissipate easily; it was trying to drown me. I kept my potential divorce hidden from most of my friends and family for months until I couldn't any longer. He was not interested in reconciliation and that fateful day of him coming to gather his belongings and leave forever was soon approaching, and so was the exposure of that truth.

Every Sunday, I would force myself to go to church and as I sat in the fifth row, center seat, it would feel like a spotlight was shining on me, exposed, as though the Pastor was talking directly to me. I felt like he knew everything I was keeping secret and was sharing my sins with the congregation, but he wasn't. I was battling the enemy in God's house. The spotlight was God's love and grace shining on me. I felt shame and guilt for hurting Him, but He would help me battle the lies of the enemy that I shouldn't be there because I was unworthy and had failed Him. I knew divorce was wrong and I was hurt for the things I knew hurt God. I didn't honestly want to be there, and I honestly did feel so unworthy, but those were the lies from the enemy. I would battle these thoughts right there in my chair during service surrounded by God's people I thought were perfect, unlike me. But in the spiritual battle, I knew God, and I knew this was where I was supposed to be. This was the "safest" place for me to be, surrounded by people who loved me and could pray for me. It wasn't easy, but I had to trust God and receive His gift of grace and forgiveness. I had to allow Him to hold my hand, carry me when I was weak and sit by my side with His people. As we sat there together one Sunday, He said to me "You are worthy to be here. This is your family. I am your Father, and these are your brothers and sisters who love you." West Community Friends Church was my family then and still is today. God was right! And if I didn't allow Him to reveal that truth to me, I'm not sure where or what my life would look like today. My church friends and family would not only support me through this difficult season but also every step ahead in my new life God had promised me! In 2003, as a single woman, I adopted a three-month-old baby boy. Several years later, I would marry my husband and together we would adopt two more baby boys that were my son's brothers. God would create a masterpiece out of war-torn canvas and use my mess to create an incredible message for us to share with others.

Through the spiritual battle and lies of the enemy, I contemplated leaving my home, my life, and running back to Colorado where I had a family. Thank God I had ears to hear the Lord speak to me, "This is your home. This is your plan. I will never leave you. I will be with you every step of the way even when it gets hard. I will remain by your side." If I would have acted on my own emotions and not listened to or obeyed God, I would not have my three amazing children or husband living our incredibly blessed life or even writing this book today. I would have missed out on my incredible, but a difficult, journey through the desert and crossing into the promised land!

As I would seek God daily, even some days hourly, sometimes minute by minute just to continue moving forward with my daily responsibilities, God would teach me His promises. One promise I learned was in Romans 8:28 which became my life verse during this time. It brought me comfort and a promise I would hold onto. It says, *"All things work together for good for those who love the Lord and called according to His purposes."* Every Friday night in my calendar, after work and racquetball with a friend, my priority was *date night with Jesus*. I would cook a delicious homemade dinner and we would sit together in the hot tub under the stars of Heaven. We would spend the entire night together talking, crying, laughing, and dreaming. I would learn from Him so many important principles for my journey. I would cry out to Him this verse and say to Him over and over, "I love you, God! That's me, Father! I love you! I know I am called according to your purposes God, and so I will trust you!" I would repeat it over and over with tears in my eyes, crying out to the Heavens above. I somehow knew in my spirit that He was already working things out for my good, even if I couldn't see it or even understand it. And believe me, I didn't feel it, see it, or even comprehend it. But God said it, so I clung to His words and chose to believe it!

"Times of refreshing come from the presence of God. Make it an ongoing lifestyle, not a one-time event." Graham Cook

Like a good friend, developing a trusting relationship requires quality time and deeply personal conversation. I encourage you to spend time in God's presence and have conversations with Him so you can learn His character and trustworthiness. You will begin to know Him well and your dependence on Him for guidance and comfort will become a natural response to choices and decisions. You will develop Jesus-like trust in your Father and be a living example of Jesus in your life. Having a relationship with Jesus is like when you first meet a new boyfriend or have a best friend. He is easy to laugh with, easy to love,

> **We must learn to seek God first as He is where we will find our knowledge and wisdom to become more like Him and the power to transform through His spirit.**

and easy to receive gifts of comfort and advice from. He is like your best friend you run to when you need to spill your guts, or cry on His shoulder, or confused about decisions you must make in your life. He is not only your protector and provider, but He is your best friend, comforter, healer, and counselor.

The relationship between Jesus and His Father is one of the most important relationships to ever exist, just as OUR relationship with the Father is to be important. We see plainly stated by Jesus Himself attributes of the perfect relationship between Father and Son in John 5:17-37. Let us look at Jesus' relationship with His Father and gleam important lessons in developing a strong relationship with our Father.

1. **Jesus reflects His Father.** Jesus works as His Father works. Jesus imitates His Father; he does what He sees His Father do. Jesus said, *"My Father is working until now and I am working"* and He also said, *"The Son can do only what he sees the Father doing."* John 5:17, 19 When we seek God, we can focus our efforts of seeking Him to immolate and reflect God's character in our lives.

2. **Jesus is dependent on His Father.** *"He can do nothing on His own accord."* John 5:19 Jesus is equal in deity, as part of the trinity, yet submissive in the role as a human being, as the Son of man, walking on earth. Jesus walks in humility before His Father and is dependent on Him for everything. When we seek God, we learn to become dependent on Him and know we are not the leader, but the follower, a daughter dependent on her daddy.

3. **Jesus has faith in His Father's love for Him.** *"For the Father loves the Son,"* Jesus says in John 5:20. This is where Jesus' security comes from. He does not put His faith in human beings' love for Him. Where His self-worth is concerned, He does not care about anyone's opinion other that His Fathers. Jesus did not entrust Himself to people. (John 2 24) His security came from His faith in His Father's love for Him. When we seek God first, our minds focus on God's love for us, and how we are perfect in His image, therefore, we can walk in purpose without fear of others' opinions and judgment.

4. **Jesus' trust and His confidence were in His Father.** *"And greater works than these will he show Him so that you may marvel."* John 5:20 Jesus was sure he could trust His Father. He trusted that the works His Father told Him were to come, that they would come. His raising Lazarus from the dead, His resurrection, and the pouring out of the Holy Spirit. These were all yet to come, but Jesus trusted and had confidence in His Father that He would be faithful to His word and promises. When we seek God, we can trust and have confidence in what He tells us and promises us in the Bible.

5. **Jesus lives for His Father's will.** *"I seek not my own will, but the will of Him who sent me."* John 5:30 He is equal in a deity as a part of the Trinity but submissive in His role. Jesus never performed a miracle on His behalf. He only became angry and defensive for God's righteousness, never on His behalf. Jesus did not live for Himself. He lived for the Father. When we seek God, our desires unite with God's heart, and we choose to live for His will.

"What you see in God, you will reflect back to Him." Graham Cook

I honestly do not know how I would have survived, let alone thrived, that season of my life if not for my relationship with Jesus and the daily communion and reassurances He gave me to keep moving forward. I was developing a relationship with my Father just as Jesus taught us in these five important lessons we just discussed. While I was broken and hurting on the inside, the world saw Jesus in me. They saw me endure pain and great sadness, but my friends and family tell me they saw His light of joy, forgiveness, and peace in me. I believed the things God told me in our intimate communion and so I lived my life as though it were true. If you seek Him, you will find Him. If you call Him, He will answer. If you need Him, He is there. If you find Him, you will find freedom.

When we seek Him, we are praying but we are doing so much more than that. We are looking at His face, looking into His eyes, sensing His heart, receiving comfort, wisdom, direction, and Kingdom perspective. Our mindset and heart change when we change our perspective and understand the power released in the *secret place with Jesus*, our priorities change, and He becomes the first place and thought where we begin and end our day.

"Our circumstances may be squeezing us, but when we seek Him, God begins to squeeze our circumstances." Graham Cook

I encourage you today to pull out your calendars and schedule time with God. Your calendar reflects your priorities and the things most important to you. They are reminders of your daily activities and commitments. Schedule time with Jesus every day and watch your wisdom grow and your life begins to bear fruit where dead trees were once rooted. He will uproot the old and replant new life within you. Your Godly character will begin to blossom and grow like a beautiful fruit tree that feeds hungry souls. It is not easy to naturally seek God first, as we have many distractions and influences in our lives including our husbands, children, family, media, and even the church. But if we put it in our calendar, it becomes a priority and therefore placing Him in the first position, priority over all other things. I encourage you to enjoy spending time in His presence as I did with my special *Friday night date nights* with Him. You will gain insight into His heart, character, and the desires of His will for your life, you will learn about His immense love for you. You will unite with His mind and heart. You will begin to live out His will as Jesus did in the Garden of Gethsemane. His life, and our life, would be completely different had Jesus not sought His Father's will at that moment but instead, managed His emotions and life by His own will and desires. But instead, He sought His Father and surrendered to His Father's will. *"Not my will God, but yours,"* Jesus said.

If we do not seek Him, we have nothing planted within us and therefore we have few resources to retrieve. However, if we choose today to prioritize our relationship with God and choose to develop the skill of seeking Him daily, we will gain a wealth of wisdom and truth to lean upon and rest well in challenging times.

At the beginning of the chapter, we focused on the definitions of seek, God, and first, but let us also be aware of their *antonyms*, the opposite of their definitions. The antonyms for "seek" are overlooked, run away, lead, lose, ignore, miss, neglect, pass by, brush aside, brush off, dismiss, and disregard. Let us be seekers of His righteousness and Kingdom, not overlookers, ignore, runaway, neglect, or dismiss Him. Antonyms for "first" are ending, final, finally, following, inessential, inferior, insignificant, minor, nonessential, trivial, and unnecessary. Let us seek Him first and not live our lives like He is our final counsel of insignificant, minor, and nonessential knowledge, but seek Him as though we know who He is, God of the universe, Creator of the Heavens and Earth, and all living things, our moral compass, and our Savior!

Just as when a contractor builds a house, He first pours the concrete foundation for the home to be built upon, we too need to pour our foundation on Christ Jesus. Without seeking Him first, we are simply living our life according to our desires and plans, not His. We are building a beautiful home with all the greatest furnishings and upgrades, but it is built on sand and *can* sink. It *can* fall. When a cement foundation dries, it is firm and difficult to move or destroy, just as our hearts and spirits become when we are cemented with the love and wisdom of Christ as *our* foundation. Jesus speaks of this truth in Matthew. We need to build our house upon a solid foundation which is the rock of Jesus Christ. Matthew 7:24-27 *"Everyone then who hears these words of mine and does them will be like a wise man who built His house on the rock. And the rain fell, and the floods came, and the winds blew and beat on that house, but it did not fall, because it had been founded on the rock. And everyone who hears these words of mine and does not do them will be like a foolish man who built His* house on the sand. And the rain fell, and the floods came, and the winds blew and beat against that house, and it fell, and great was the fall of it."

Again, in Matthew 6:33 it says, *"But seek first His Kingdom and His righteousness, and these things will be given to you as well."* He reminds you that when you seek Him and His righteousness first, He gives you all things of His heart. He fine-tunes your thoughts and synchronizes them with His thoughts, and you desire what He desires. Remember, when Jesus sought His Father in the Garden of Gethsemane, it began as wanting another way out of His troubles, but His heart gave way to what God's plan and His will were for His life. This is what happens to your desires when you seek Him first, your heart and thoughts will become united with His and you start living and walking in His will.

Ladies, I tell you my story to help you prepare for *your story*. It was not easy, but it was possible to be broken and shattered and yet live my life with hope and joy of the promises found in Jeremiah 29:11, *"For I know the plans I have for you,"* declares the Lord. *"Plans to prosper you and not harm you, but to give you hope and a future."*. This was another of my other life verses through that season. I was given a gift with this verse on it, and it hung on my bathroom wall for years as I read it every day, and God's spirit engraved it upon my heart. If He said it, I could believe it! He did not want to harm me! He wanted me to prosper and have hope! He had a plan for my life! And here I am today, sharing my story with you as I pray that God will speak to you, and you too will learn His amazing plans for your life!

"Prayer and rejoicing with God are not optional, it is necessary."
Graham Cook

Ask yourself these questions: "Will you be prepared for life's hardships?" "How do you prepare today for tomorrow's trouble?" "Where do you seek your truth?" "Did you seek Jesus first for your truth?" "Where do you go when you need help? Comfort? Healing?" Jeremiah 29:13 says, *"You will seek Me and find Me when you seek Me with all your heart."* The simple answer is to **Seek God today, tomorrow, and every day. Seek God first!** Seek wisely as though your entire life depends upon it. Because it does! YOUR ENTIRE LIFE DEPENDS ON SEEKING GOD FIRST.

Here is another acronym I use to remind myself of *how to* seek Him and what I *can expect* to find when I SEEK God:

S=Surrender and Search for Him in the Secret place.
E=Engage and Expect Him to reveal Himself to you.
E=Experience His love for you and Execute His plans for your life.
K=Kinship to the King is discovered and it will empower you to live like Jesus.

"If you fail to plan, you are planning to fail." Benjamin Franklin.*"* So, let's make a plan to *Seek God* First so we do not fail! Here are some practical steps to create and plan intimate time with God:

1. **IDENTIFY A TIME AND LOCATION WITH HIM**
   - Choose a time that works in your calendar that will be a consistent day and time. For some, it is morning, and others, it is better in the evening. Choose wisely based on your life.
   - Schedule your time with God in your calendar. Make it an appointment and a priority. Write it down in the calendar. Create a habit. Create a significant date or event with Him.
   - Use the time like a friend, not a mandate, but an opportunity to get to know Him.
   - Choose a consistent place, venue, and location to meet with Him. Make it special, like a date to enjoy.

2. **CREATE AN ATMOSPHERE AND INVITE HIS PRESENCE IN**
   - Worship and praise Him daily with a song or in prayer.
   - Quiet your spirit in silence and prepare your heart to listen for your Father's voice. The more you turn down the volume of the world and your mind, the more tuned in His voice becomes.
   - Quiet your soul, close your eyes and invite the Holy Spirit to dwell with you.
   - Ask Him to reveal Himself to you; speak, see, and hear the things of the Spirit world.

3. **ACTIVATE YOUR PLAN**
   - Read His word daily. Do not overwhelm yourself, just read a chapter a day until you form a habit and God leads you to more.
   - Start with Proverbs and read one every day before prayer.
   - Journal your thoughts and hearts down on paper before you seek Him. This will help you to release worries, plans, and the day's activities before synchronizing your spirit with His.
   - Use your journal daily to write your concerns, troubles, decisions, and victories you would like to discuss with Him.
   - Ask Him directly about your questions and then pause and be silent. Ask Him to speak with you.
   - Write everything you hear in your journal so you can read, meditate, and reflect on His truths and desires for your life.
   - Read God's word and scriptures for promises He is giving you that speak to you regarding your life and circumstances.

4. **REVIEW YOUR JOURNAL OFTEN TO GET CONFIRMATIONS AND AFFIRMATIONS**
   - Read your journal often to see what guidance He has given you, what wisdom you are listening to and where He was right.
   - Read your journal often to see which of God's promises are being fulfilled. Write down the date next to His instructions or insight that have manifested or been resolved through prayer.
   - Watch for God's signs of obedience and blessings throughout your day.

I pray that this chapter has given you a glimpse of inspiration and encouragement to seek God first. It is a skill that can be developed and strengthened by the simple act of prioritizing Him every morning as you open your eyes. Go to God first in counsel and ask Him to bless your day and to give you the wisdom and desire to follow Him closely all day long. He is with you. He is *Immanuel*; God with you. I pray as you continue to seek Him for next week, He will reveal new and powerful wisdom to you. That will be exactly what you need for the circumstances you face today.

Group Discussion Questions:

1. How did Jesus spend His time with His Father? When and where? Why? Discuss with the group.

2. I talked about my date night with Jesus and how important it was to my life and healing. Do you have a special time you meet with Jesus? When and where?

3. Have you thought or done something you thought was of God but later learned it was not? Write it down, seek God together in your group and pray for forgiveness and direction.

4. Jesus endured trials but maintained stability and steadiness with His life and God's purposes for His life. How can you find stability in difficult circumstances and trials?

5. What is God telling you is your priority as a mom? A wife? Sister or daughter? Leader, home manager, or at church? Pray often and ask Him to direct you or redirect you as needed.

6. Are you where you are supposed to be? How can you be certain? When did you last seek God for His purposes in your life?

7. Write out the scripture Mathew 6:33. Discuss what this verse means to you personally after learning about it in this lesson.

Homework:

1. Have you forgotten to seek God first and found yourself suffering from your own choices and decisions? Identify and write down those circumstances and consequences.

2. Open your calendars and identify the best days and times to meet with Jesus every day. Make it 30 minutes a day until you become comfortable and confident with your commitment. What is your plan?

3. Why do you think Jesus prayed every day? Alone? And why did He seek His Father mostly in the morning?

4. What things get in your way every day? Explain.

   _____
   _____
   _____
   _____
   _____

5. What would you have to arrange in your schedule to develop this characteristic like Jesus?

   _____
   _____
   _____
   _____
   _____

6. What do you think would change for you in your life if you developed this characteristic? Be specific and give several examples of work, home, family, relationships, finances.

   _____
   _____
   _____
   _____
   _____

7. Calendar your time. Pull out your calendar now and add Him in every day, week, and month. Share it with a friend.

   _____
   _____
   _____
   _____
   _____

Daily Prayer to Develop this Characteristic:

Dear Heavenly Father, you are the creator of my life and you have designed me to seek you first before all things. Lord, help me to prioritize you before I start my day, make decisions, make plans, choose all things in my life. I love you Lord and surrender my will in exchange for yours. I want your Holy Spirit to transform my life to reflect that of Jesus Christ by seeking your vision, desires, and priorities through all things. Help me see you more clearly and to trust your love for me. I give you my heart and put my trust in you from this day forward. Change me, mold me, shape me into a godly woman who seeks you first in all things every day.

<u>Journal Your Own Prayer:</u>

Godly Characteristic #2
Unconditional Love

Jesus replied: "'Love the Lord your God with all your heart and with all your soul and with all your mind. This is the first and greatest commandment. And the second is like it: Love your neighbor as yourself."

Matthew 22:37-39

Lori Bryant

Water of Life Church, Fontana CA

Lori Bryant's Stories and Art with a Voice Ministry

Lori Bryant is an author, speaker, poet, and inspirational storyteller. She has a unique way of using story, poetry, and art to convey the Father's love to all people. Her passion is to help others find healing, and freedom to live their lives to the fullest. She and her husband Bob spent the past 30 years ministering to families and the next generation with a message of hope and restoration.

Lori is the mother of two daughters and three sons. She and Bob were promoted to "Grand" parents. Bob transitioned to his eternal home on November 30th, 2020. Lori is figuring out her new life as a widow while maintaining Bob's legacy. Lori is currently a Minister on staff in the Healing and Caring Department at Water of Life Church in Fontana, CA. She is the Director of their healing rooms prayer ministry associated with Healing Rooms International healing prayer ministry. Along with her long-time friend Danielle Jones, Lori founded the ministry Art with A Voice. Lori taught Positively Transforming Women's Ministry. Lori also enjoys speaking at women's retreats, events, and conferences at various churches, and other organizations. She and Bob loved international missions. She also has been involved with outreach all around the world.

Lori is a frequent contributor to the Chicken Soup for the Soul series. She has contributed her stories to Zoe Life devotionals. She has taught a monthly writer's workshop where she teaches others how to successfully author their own stories. She has also facilitated two books with short stories from herself and other authors.

You can contact Lori at Lobrya9@aol.com, or on Facebook at Lori Bryant's Stories and Art with A Voice.

Unconditional Love

Jesus replied: *"Love the Lord your God with all your heart and with all your soul and with all your mind. This is the first and greatest commandment. And the second is like it: 'Love your neighbor as yourself.' All the Law and the Prophets hang on these two commandments."* Matthew 22:37-40

Jesus was approached by an expert in the law, a Pharisee. He did not have His attorney represent Him. He knew the past, present, and future, He knew the answer. Moses began with ten commandments. The Jewish leaders added 603 laws, and the New Testament gives us 1050 commandments, but Jesus narrowed it down to one, "Love", love God, and love people. In 1 Corinthians it tells us *"Only faith, hope, and love remain but the greatest of these is love!"*

Luke 14: 12-14 Then Jesus also said to His host, *"When you give a dinner or a supper, do not ask your friends, your brothers, your relatives, nor rich neighbors, lest they also invite you back, and you be repaid. But when you give a feast, invite the poor, the maimed, the lame, the blind. And you will be blessed because they cannot repay you; for you shall be repaid at the resurrection of the just."*

I was scared, excited, and in tremendous pain. Saint Patrick's Day 1982, I was only 19 years old. "One more good push and the baby will be here." My doctor pronounced from the foot of the bed. "Come on, you can do this." Standing by were pediatric doctors and neonatal nurses. There were incubators, oxygen tanks, machines, and devices that I had never seen in my lifetime. The delivery room was packed and ready. My baby was about to be born, almost 6 weeks early.

Finally, one of the doctors said, "Congratulations it's a girl!" A brief look at my tiny daughter and a whirlwind of activity began. I could tell right away that something was wrong. The nurse attending to my baby was serious and concerned. The pediatrician started barking orders at everyone "They must take the baby now. You can see her in a little while." "Is something wrong?" I asked, "Don't worry, she is in good hands." Why did this not ease my mind?

The next morning a large and happy nurse brought Mellissa to my room for a quick visit. She was just under five pounds and wrapped like a little burrito. I was afraid to hold her. I asked the nurse, "Where is the rest of her?" She laughed aloud and said, "Honey, that's all you gave us and that's all you get back!" She reached out and handed her to me. Instantly, I fell deeply in love with my tiny daughter. She was so beautiful, her jet-black hair and little pink pouty lips. I cried again only this time out of overwhelming love and thankfulness. She opened her eyes slightly and looked at me. "I love you, Mellissa." I whispered to her through my tears, "We are going to be okay; everything will be okay. You don't know me yet, but I am your mom and I love you more than anything."

It is no wonder that God chose to call Himself Father. It is one of the best examples of *agape love*. The love of a parent towards a newborn requires no effort at all on the part of the baby. It is a deep one-way love relationship. The very existence of the child is all that is required for the love of the parent to be given.

I remember wondering when I was pregnant with my second child, "How will I love like that again?" The moment that He was born there it was. The love that I felt for my son was not divided into two kinds of love but a big, real, brand-new love! When my third child was born, I could not believe it really happened again. As I anticipated the birth of my fourth baby, I fully expected it. God in His infinite love does the same for each one of us. He does not give us each a portion of love and affection, He gives it all, all the time.

"Unconditional love" in the dictionary is characterized as this; is known as affection without any limitations or love without conditions. In psychology, unconditional love refers to a state of mind in which one has the goal of increasing the welfare of another, despite any evidence of benefit for oneself. When we love unconditionally, it means that we love people in tough times. This means loving someone when they are being self-consumed or inconsiderate. It also means loving those who hate us, loving our enemies. Unconditional love is, without doubt, a Godly characteristic and not a natural human characteristic.

Dr. Emerson Eggerich, the author of Love and Respect, put it this way. "To love unconditionally, we obey God's command to put on love and respect despite the circumstances" (Romans 12:10; 1 Peter 2:17). "If we refuse to obey this command, we end up rationalizing (telling ourselves "rational lies") and believing others have caused us to be harsh and rude. We tell others, in numerous ways, they made us react the way we did."

When my kids were all teenagers, I noticed myself becoming frustrated, angry and controlling. I was reacting to their moods, emotions, and behavior. I was defiantly not responding in peace or love. One day I cried out to the Lord, "Change the way my kids are thinking and behaving. I feel like I am losing it! I would be the best mom on the planet if they would only do what I say!"

To my surprise, I felt a quiet response inside of me. "If their behavior changes you, changes your love, something is wrong with you not them." Realizing that the only person I can truly control is me and I cannot even do that well most of the time.

I desire to remain consistent in love, immersed in peace, fully open to the voice of God. I long for a constant awareness of my thoughts and choices. I pray each morning that I would choose joy, focus on everything good, see the best in others and continue to surrender to the Lord and His love. This is not a natural state of being but a supernatural connection to the Holy Spirit. It is a realization for me that I am the only one that I need to work on and at any given moment I have many choices. I know that after fifty-six years I am still a work in progress.

In Matthew 5: 43-48, we learn *"You have heard that it was said, 'You shall love your neighbor and hate your enemy but I say to you, love your enemies, bless those who curse you, do good to those who hate you and pray for those who spitefully use you and persecute you, that you may be sons of your Father in heaven; for He makes His sun rise on the evil and the good, and sends rain on the just and on the unjust. For if you love those who love you, what reward have you? Do not even the tax collectors do the same? And if you greet your brethren only, what do you do more than others? Therefore, you shall be perfect, just as your Father in heaven is perfect."*

As if unconditional love is not enough? Jesus always takes it up a notch! He washes the feet of His betrayer, forgives the crucifier with the hammer in his hand, and shows amazing grace to the woman caught in adultery. He asked the Father to forgive His accusers saying they know not what they do. He honored the outcasts of His time, the poor, the sick, lame and broken. He ate with sinners and tax collectors. He walked in compassion so fully that crowds of people followed Him wherever He went knowing that healing was possible in His very presence. Jesus liberated women with His new covenant and called for all men to be free.

I especially love the story of His encounter with the woman at the well. She was so beaten down with shame and regret having no real hope for her healing or for her value to be restored. She was unable to pursue Him, so He encountered her. To her complete surprise, she was known by God, loved, and set free that day. One encounter with God and she was redeemed, forgiven, and restored. The Bible tells us that she became an evangelist to her whole town testifying of the love and power of Jesus. He laid down His own life for you and me while we were enemies of God long before we ever said yes to Him. When we were not pursuing God, He was always pursuing us.

One of my favorite human examples of this in the Bible is Daniel. Daniel and his friends were kidnapped, enslaved, and forced to serve one of the evilest kings in history, King Nebuchadnezzar. He was referred to as the destroyer of nations. Daniel was taken from his culture, home, and family into captivity. Despite these extremely difficult circumstances Daniel was able to honor God and honor the king. On at least two accounts King Nebuchadnezzar was about to put Daniel to death and God intervened to save him.

The time comes that Daniel interprets the king's dream, the dream he had of his demise in verse nineteen in the book of Daniel. I would have at least thought to myself if I were Daniel, that the king is about to get what He has deserved all along and I am so glad that I get to tell him. Daniel replies in love, *"My Lord if only the dream applied to your enemies and its meaning to your adversaries!"* (Not to you). After all that Daniel and his people had been through because of Nebuchadnezzar, Daniel shows love and compassion instead of revenge.

How little it takes to anger most of us. Offense and unforgiveness take over in our own families. Our news is full of stories of rage, murder, and hate. How sad to see the church in the same condition? We experience church splits, divorce, dishonor, and divisions of all kinds. Unfortunately, we have become more known for what we are against, who we do not like, and where we have drawn lines.

Would not it be world-changing if we simply connected to the Father as Jesus did? If we did what He did and said what He said, we would be known for God's powerful healing and redeeming love. Compassion would rule our lives and people would be drawn to us seeing a full demonstration of who God really is.

I remember a day, not that long ago. I was driving with a friend. I looked straight ahead as we drove and said, "I have to confess something to you." I then proceeded to tell her how much hatred I had for someone that was hurting my family with little concern. I went on, "I have tried everything I can think of to forgive. I have done everything that I would tell someone else to do, nothing is working! I hate them and they just keep causing more pain!"

My friend shook her head and said, "I've never seen your face do that before Lori." The truth is I had never felt this stuck in anger and unforgiveness. I want to say I have forgiven them and wish them well, but I know that is not true. I cannot take it anymore. I told her, "I can't carry the weight of this anymore. I am exhausted."

I think that just saying it aloud to someone else was helpful. I mean loving the people who love you back is hard enough sometimes but loving those who have hurt you, persecuted you, caused heartache to the ones you love most, is impossible without the love and understanding of God.

The truth is apart from God no one can do it. We are talking about a supernatural work of the Holy Spirit in us. I think that is the point. Love God is the first part of the commandment because we must spend time with Him in His presence and His word. We must let Him transform us, humble us, and help us see people from His perspective. It comes down to trust, trusting God to be who He says He is, trusting Him to do all that He says He can do. Letting go of my rights and judgments.

My friend finally answered, "Lori, are you ready to be ready to forgive? I think that's what God wants." Ready to be ready? Yes, I think willing, willing to love, willing to forgive, and willing to surrender my way to His way is the pathway to surrender…surrendering to love.

I prayed a prayer not so long ago, "Lord let me love deeper. Let me love people as you do." I just did not expect Him to answer by bringing so many rude, mean, and hard-to-love people into my life. It is kind of like; everyone wants to see miracles but not many want to hang around the people who need them. There is a cost to be paid, do I really want it? Am I willing to pay?

> **Would not it be world changing if we simply connected to the Father like Jesus did. If we did what He did and said what He said, we would be known for God's powerful healing and redeeming love.**

In Luke 7:36-48, we learn a story about Jesus being anointed by a sinful woman. It teaches us *"When one of the Pharisees invited Jesus to have dinner with Him, He went to the Pharisee's house and reclined at the table. A woman in that town who lived a sinful life learned that*

Jesus was eating at the Pharisee's house, so she came there with an alabaster jar of perfume. As she stood behind Him at His feet weeping, she began to wet His feet with her tears. Then she wiped them with her hair, kissed them, and poured perfume on them. When the Pharisee who had invited Him saw this, He said to himself, "If this man were a prophet, He would know who is touching Him and what kind of woman she is—that she is a sinner." Jesus answered Him, "Simon, I have something to tell you." "Tell me, teacher," he said. "Two people owed money to a certain moneylender. One owed Him five hundred denarii, and the other fifty. Neither of them had the money to pay Him back, so He forgave the debts of both. Now which of them will love Him more?" Simon replied, "I suppose the one who had the bigger debt forgiven." You have judged correctly," Jesus said. Then He turned toward the woman and said to Simon, "Do you see this woman? I came into your house. You did not give me any water for my feet, but she wet my feet with her tears and wiped them with her hair. You did not kiss me, but this woman, from the time I entered, has not stopped kissing my feet. You did not put oil on my head, but she has poured perfume on my feet. Therefore, I tell you, her many sins have been forgiven—as her great love has shown. But whoever has been forgiven little loves little." Then Jesus said to her, "Your sins are forgiven."

We learn that Jesus loves the sinner, and we are called to be like Jesus. We are created in God's image and His desire is for us to live a righteous and holy life and display the Godly characteristic of love in us and through us. My prayer for you today is that you will have a glimpse of God's love for you and because He first loved us, we can love others unconditionally. You will have to develop this characteristic and mature in it to be increasingly like Jesus. But we can walk in love like Jesus.

My perspective on life and people has changed so dramatically as I pursue God's love for us, and I understand His desire for us to walk fully in His love so we can share His love with others.

"Seek Him and you will find Him. Ask and it will be given to you. Knock and He will answer." While this in Matthew 7:7 is referring to receiving God's grace and salvation for you, we can use this concept with receiving the gift of His Godly characteristic. Seek Him and you

will find His love. Ask and His love will be given to you. Knock and He will answer you. God is love.

Remember the statistics I quoted at the beginning of this chapter about the laws and commandments? Well, the most important one was not quoted or written by a Pharisee or teacher of the law, but by our most loving teacher Jesus. He said, *"To love God above all things and love your neighbor."* We find it in many places in scripture. Love is the most important thing to our Father.

Luke 10:27 *He answered, "'Love the LORD your God with all your heart and with all your soul and with all your strength and with all your mind'; and 'Love your neighbor as yourself.'"*

Mark 12:30-31 *"Love the LORD your God with all your heart and with all your soul and with all your mind and with all your strength." The second is this: 'Love your neighbor as yourself.' There is no commandment greater than these."*

Deuteronomy 6:5 *"Love the LORD your God with all your heart and with all your soul and with all your strength."*

Leviticus 19:18 *"'Do not seek revenge or bear a grudge against anyone among your people but love your neighbor as yourself. I am the LORD."*

Let us begin today to walk in the fullness and supernatural power and love of Jesus. People will see us, and they will know God by our love. John 13:35 *"Let me give you a new command: Love one another. In the same way, I loved you, you love one another. This is how everyone will recognize that you are my disciples—when they see the love you have for each other."*

Group Discussion Questions:

1. You heard me tell you I cried out to God one day "Lord let me love deeper. Let me love people as you do." Share with your group if you have ever cried this out to God. Share what it was like and what happened.

2. I just did not expect Him to answer by bringing so many rude, mean, and hard-to-love people into my life! It is kind of like; everyone wants to see miracles but not many want to hang around the people who need them. Can you relate? Share when and how.

3. There is a cost to be paid when we desire to live in the Godly characteristic of unconditional love. Ask yourself these questions: Do I really want it? Am I willing to pay? Share with the group.

4. "I have done everything that I would tell someone else to do, nothing is working! I hate them and they just keep causing more pain!" Have you felt this way? Are you ready to be ready to forgive? Share with the group your response.

5. When did you first realize that it is hard to naturally love people, but only through the love of God can you supernaturally love others unconditionally? Share with the group.

Homework:

1. What are some tangible ways that you can gaze into the Gospel every single day and spend time in God's love to get His perspective on love? Write those tangible ways and begin to form a habit so you can mature in the Godly characteristic of unconditional love.

   _____
   _____
   _____
   _____

2. Did those moments cause you to gain any new perspective on yourself?

   _____
   _____
   _____
   _____

3. What messages have been ingrained in you that keep you from really believing that God could love you and that He has placed His unconditional love in you to love others that way too?

   _____
   _____
   _____
   _____

4. Share a time that you felt unconditional love for an enemy or someone who had hurt you deeply? Write about your experience of how the Holy Spirit was alive in you.

   _____
   _____
   _____
   _____

Daily Prayer to Develop this Characteristic:

Father God, I recognize and declare that YOU ARE LOVE! God, I know that you love me and that you have placed deep within me your amazing love and grace for your people. Father, I pray that you would reveal that supernatural love to me and help me daily to develop it and mature in it as I seek after you. Father, forgive me for the times I respond to others in hate or bitterness and cleanse my heart of the negative emotions of this world. Restore my heart and my love for everyone around me that needs to know your love and yet, thank you for using me as that vehicle to show the Father. I ask that you make me bold in my convictions of your love and that I would reflect that amazing unconditional love to the world. In Jesus' name. Amen.

Journal Your Own Prayer:

Godly Characteristic #3
Prayerful Life

Jesus said "Call to me and I will answer you and tell you. great and mighty things you do not know."

Jeremiah 33:3

Esther Rose Neal
Celebration Church OC,
San Juan Capistrano CA
Worship Leader, Songwriter,
Recording Artist
Freedom Tents Ministry

Esther Rose Neal is a worship leader, singer/songwriter, recording artist, and speaker. She is the wife of Rich Neal and mom of a beautiful miracle daughter Shiloh.

My burning heart's desire is for people to be set free, healed, restored, brought into their true identity and purpose through the power of God's presence and love. I minister through encouraging teaching, personal testimonies, prophecy, and prayer. I am a worship leader and director at Celebration Church OC in San Juan Capistrano, CA. I am also raising up other worship leaders to flow in power and freedom.

I have shared on different radio and television programs, churches, conferences, ministries, outreaches, and more. God has been using me in pastoral and worship leader gatherings. I started Freedom Tents Outreach Ministry to take God's presence out to people everywhere. God is bringing revival and a great harvest which will set people free to come into true identity and will bring us into perfect unity to shine for God's glory upon the earth!

For more information or to contact Esther Rose Neal visit: www.EstherRoseNeal.com or email me at estherroseneal@gmail.com.

Prayerful Life

The Webster dictionary defines the word "prayer" as a form of connection and communication between you and God. Together, we will explore prayer as a lifeline, life-giving, and a Godly characteristic. We will seek God and ask Him to help us become more like Jesus in our prayer life.

I would have never called myself a prayer warrior, and to tell you the truth, I did not feel qualified to write about the Godly characteristic of prayer. Yet, as I began to pray about what God would have me share with you on His behalf, God began to open my eyes to what prayer looks like in my life.

I try to talk with God all day long. Usually, it's me saying "HELP! I NEED YOU FOR EVERYTHING!" But really, it is just me trying to keep myself open to His heart and leading and sharing my heart and needs with Him day by day, and sometimes moment by moment. I love the verse Philippians 4:6, *"Don't be pulled in different directions or worried about a thing. Be saturated in prayer throughout each day, offering your faith-filled requests before God with overflowing gratitude. Tell Him every detail of your life."*

Prayer is a gift God gave us for an intimate relationship with Him. Even Jesus who was God in the flesh felt it necessary and important to regularly spend time praying and connecting with the Father. That is a big encouragement about the importance of prayer and connection.

Jesus said *"I am the vine; you are the branches. If you remain in me and I in you, you will bear much fruit; apart from me you can do nothing."* John 15:5

Jesus would frequently go away to a quiet place alone to talk to the Father. *"Before daybreak the next morning, Jesus got up and went to an isolated place to pray."* Mark 1:35

I want to encourage you on your prayer journey by sharing some ways that I pray and connect with God in the hope and expectation that it will give you the freedom to find that connection for yourself and grow in maturity with your Godly characteristic and mirror the life of Jesus.

I am a worshiper, so it is not surprising that a huge way I connect and communicate with God is through songs. Worship is a continual back and forth expression of love and revelation. As I worship, God will put people, cities, even nations on my heart to sing out in intercession. He will also reveal His heart for me in a very intimate and personal way that allows me to connect even deeper with Him and communicate my gratitude and expression back.

In the Bible, David spent much time connecting and pouring out His heart to God through songs and poetic prayers as we see throughout the Psalms. God even called David a man after His own heart. From being a shepherd to the king's musician, a fugitive, to the King himself, David needed God's guidance, strength, and friendship. This is true for us too.

God cares about us and wants us to come to Him with everything. He invites us to *"Come boldly to the throne of our gracious God. There we will receive His mercy, and we will find grace to help us when we need it most."* Hebrews 4:16. When we do that, we begin to experience intimacy with God.

True intimacy is developed from a relationship where we feel safe and loved. We get a glimpse into the intimacy and love David had with God in Psalms 27:4, *"Here's the one thing I crave from God, the one thing I seek above all else: I want the privilege of living with Him every moment in His house, finding the sweet loveliness of His face, filled with awe, delighting in His glory and grace. I want to live my life so close to Him that He takes pleasure in my every prayer."*

Prayer is not a duty but a beautiful way we feel close to God and His voice. Did you know that God sings songs over you? Did you know He prays for you? He is continually making intercession for us and is our great advocate. (1 John 2:1) He sings songs of deliverance over you, setting you free. (Psalm 32:7) Wow!

Jesus said He did what He saw the Father doing. When we invite Him into our hearts and lives, we are filled with His Spirit so we can do the same. You are empowered to pray. You are not disqualified! It is not by what you have done or not done, it is simply because of what He has done for us and His great love for us that you can connect with Him through His spirit. Because of His love for us, we have the power and Heavenly anointing upon our lives to intercede for the things of this world.

Intercessory prayer is an opportunity to align our hearts with God's and to pray for others, for nations, for circumstances, and the things of this world to shift and come into Heaven's Kingdom reality and fullness. Many times, in the Bible, prayer changed things dramatically. Maybe you have been discouraged at times and thought your prayers did not affect you much, but your prayers are powerful! It is about releasing those prayers and trusting God will do the work.

You may be thinking that you have no time to pray, let alone worship, intercede, or build intimacy with Jesus. But all He wants from you is your desire to seek Him and to trust in Him. The amount of time will change with the seasons, but His love for you will never change.

I pray a lot in the car or when I am in bed. These are places I can sometimes be alone and spend time talking with God. It is not about the when or the how, it is about simply coming to the conversation. I find the important, and necessary, time I have in prayer will make me more empowered and productive for everything else on my calendar and that I will face each day. Once I have sought Him out for strength to walk out the day, I find my days are always more peaceful, and I do not get shaken by the world's troubles.

Another way I love to pray is to walk and talk with God in nature. I sometimes go to the park and ask Holy Spirit to lead me and talk to me through His creation. It always blows me away how God speaks and reveals Himself to me in these times. It becomes a beautiful heart-to-heart exchange, and I usually leave feeling more connected and filled up than when I started. That is the purpose of prayer. Not just to share a list of requests, but to be more connected with our Father, King Jesus, and Holy Spirit. It is ok to have conversations with all three since they are all part of the Godhead. Each carries a unique and beautiful role in our lives.

I also recently discovered a new model of prayer called "Soaking prayer." This is an immensely helpful tool for listening to God because conversation does not usually work well if it is one-sided. Both are needed for strong connection and intimacy. The God of all creation, our Savior, the lover of our soul, our helper, our healer, our strength, and our Father, has valuable things to share with us.

> **Intercessory prayer is an opportunity to align our hearts with God's to pray for others, for nations, for circumstances and the things of this world to shift and come into Heaven's Kingdom reality and fullness now.**

This works in my life often and it refreshes my soul with God's perspective and love for me. I find good soaking worship instrumental songs to listen to online through my phone. I try to go to an area of my home where I can lay down without distraction. Depending on the season, this could be five minutes, thirty minutes, or an hour, whatever is available. I lay there and try to focus my heart, mind, and internal vision on God. I thank Him for who He is and focus my thoughts and vision on Him. It can help to think upon a verse or promise from scripture. Also, to ask Him a specific question or for a specific revelation. Some examples: Father, tell me how much you love me? Father, show me how you see me?

I then try to quiet myself to rest and receive in His presence. Sometimes it can be a struggle, but it is worth the time and worth the simple effort. Out of these times of quiet focused intimacy, I have seen beautiful visions that revealed God's love for me which has brought much healing.

I have received melodies and songs that flow from that heart connection. I also can feel God's heart for others, which allows my prayer life and specific prayers to be from a more authentic place by seeing others through God's eyes. It is also okay to simply rest in God's presence and take a nap. Lord knows the value of us crawling up onto our Heavenly Daddy's arms and simply resting in His love and presence.

Also, as we grow in intimacy, listening becomes such a valuable part of prayer and grows our confidence in hearing God's voice. God speaks in so many ways and will speak in ways He knows you will hear. It may be through a scripture or a vision, a simple word, or even a dream.

As we recognize His voice more, it leads to so many powerful opportunities to receive encouragement for ourselves and to minister to others. God has used this powerfully in my life. I will always have my ears open to His voice as I am worshiping because I desire to share the songs, He sings over us from His heart. This has brought so much healing to others simply by my confidence and willingness to step out in faith and release what I hear.

Likewise, when I am praying for others or ministering to them, I will listen and ask Holy Spirit to give me a vision, a song, or a word of encouragement for them. It blows me away when something that seems so insignificant to me or just a simple thought can be profound for them. God is speaking and is looking for daughters and friends who will listen.

Samuel learned to hear God's voice, but it took Eli to help Him recognize it. I want to be that encouragement to you. 1 Samuel 3:10 *"And the Lord came and called as before, "Samuel! Samuel!" And Samuel replied, "Speak, your servant is listening."*

There also may be a time when someone needs prayer for physical healing. This can be intimidating, but remember God is the one who does the healing. We are the vessel who He gives authority to pray for healing. Jesus modeled this in many ways. Some things were prevalent, like how He was filled with compassion when He saw the people in need of healing.

Compassion releases God's heart for that person and their situation. Ask God to fill you with compassion when you pray for others. That even if they do not receive their physical healing this time, they would feel His love for them. Mark 1:41-42 *"Moved with compassion, Jesus reached out and touched Him. 'I am willing. He spoke. 'Be healed!' Instantly leprosy disappeared, and the man was healed."*

My husband Rich does this every day of His life, wherever He goes. He steps out in faith and prays for others, filled with God's compassion, and has seen God heal many people and has seen them encounter His love and presence like never before. This has radically encouraged me to try and do the same. I encourage you to read and study all the healing scriptures in the Bible. God is the same yesterday, today, and forever.

Another powerful prayer tool God has used in my prayer life is called "Immanuel Prayer." Immanuel simply means *God with us* and so this Immanuel prayer is a prayer where we encounter the truth that God is always with us. This powerful prayer becomes an experience of meeting Him and seeing Him with you in your life and circumstances. You get to experience Immanuel when you learn to practice this skill of prayer in your own life.

This has brought me amazing encouragement, revelation, healing, and guidance. It is a form of prayer journaling and conversation. The Psalms in the Bible are a wonderful example of this. I will usually start by writing down a thought of gratitude or thanksgiving or a memory of joy and give Him thanks for that special memory. I then begin to ask Jesus where He was in that time and what He wants to reveal to me about the memory or gratitude I have written Him. It is amazing what you will hear and see. This will help you to further get connected in your heart and prayer life with Him.

Then you can write down more prayers, questions, and further thanks. Ask for His heart in response. Try to write down what you hear without analyzing or editing. God is speaking louder than you know and will help reveal to you what is from Him and what is not. I cannot tell you how many times this has radically blessed me! I pray you will commit your journey of living out this Godly characteristic of prayer by learning to Immanuel prayer and journaling.

God also helps give us language to pray in His word. As I read the scriptures, I will find truth or a promise and begin praying that over myself, my family, and others. I will sometimes make a little note and date on it so I can look back and remember prayers and desires. Also, to see how I can continue to pray or how they have already been answered.

There are so many promises in His word for us. We can declare and receive those from our good Father as He wills. All His promises are yes and amen through Christ Jesus! There also can be times and situations in life that will be exceedingly difficult. The Bible character

Hannah prayed with an inner groaning and with tears in the temple at Shiloh as she prayed and longed for a child as described in 1 Samuel 1.

God hears our pain and heart's desires. I longed for a child and went through two miscarriages, which was a deep loss for me each time. I sometimes did not know how to even express my prayers and desires to God in my pain and disappointment. Yet He heard my heart and longing and stored up all my tears. He sent me on a journey I never would have expected but He kept asking me to trust Him in every step. He even spoke these verses to me in the emergency room when I was going through my second miscarriage. Proverbs 3:5-6 *"Trust in the Lord with all your heart and lean not on your own understanding; In all your ways acknowledge Him, And He shall direct your paths."*

I did choose to trust Him and now I have a beautiful daughter named Shiloh. She is my special miracle gift from God. It was at Shiloh where Hannah cried out for a child and God gave her Samuel. The Lord hears our cries and cares for us. 1 Peter 5:7 says, *"Give all your worries and cares to God, for He cares about you."*

The Holy Spirit even helps pray for us in our times of weakness. And the Holy Spirit helps us in our weakness. For example, Romans 8:26 tells us, *"We do not know what God wants us to pray for, but the Holy Spirit prays for us with groanings that cannot be expressed in words."* Let us be grateful to our God who is always with us and is for us.

Now let us learn about *prayer and fasting* through this amazing woman of God in the Bible, Esther. She became a prayer warrior that sought the Lord through prayer and fasting when she was faced with a life and death situation, not only for herself and her family but for an entire nation of people. She also asked others to fast for her. It is so amazing to have others praying with and for you! We are not meant to do this life and journey alone.

Esther 4:16 *"Go and gather together all the Jews of Susa together and fast for me. Do not eat or drink for three days, night or day. My maids and I will do the same. And then, thou it is against the law, I will go in to see the king. If I must die, I must die."* Prayer and fasting prepared Esther for the greatest spiritual battle and victory of her life and she used the power of unity and agreement with others to join her in this battle. Jesus even fasted forty days and nights before the enemy came to try and tempt Him before He began His public ministry.

Fasting is not something I have done regularly, but there have been pivotal times in my life when it was especially important to do. I do not know all that fasting does, but I do believe it helps get our hearts and vision even more sensitive to the Lord's since we are denying our flesh.

The enemy must not like it since He has been tempting the things of our flesh from the start with Adam and Eve. When we deny our flesh, it brings a greater authority to come against the things of the enemy and to come into agreement with God. An example of this is when Jesus delivers a boy of a demon and tells His disciples when asked why they were unable to cast it out? Mark 9:29 *He said to them, "This kind can come out only by prayer and fasting."*

If Jesus, did it and shared a value for it, then it is something to pray and ask God for, ask Him for the grace to do as He places it on your heart. There are many ways to fast. You can fast a meal, one item that is a sacrifice, like sugar or chocolate, a Daniel fast, etc. It is about giving that time, affection, and attention to God.

I know some of these ways of praying might be brand new to you and outside of your comfort zone. My heart is that you would be encouraged and that the paradigm or box of what you thought prayer had to look like would be broken and enlarged. The main point of prayer is for you to connect and communicate with the one who loves you most, the King of all kings, your everlasting Father, your comfort, and your guide.

There is no shame, simply an invitation to intimacy. It is an invitation to lean upon the chest of your Heavenly Father and be set free to know His voice and believe that He loves hearing yours and will be there when you call upon His name. No prayer is too big or small, He just wants you to come. Out of this, you will discover a deeper connection to God and His voice than you ever thought possible.

We were created in the beginning to walk and talk with God in the garden. Jesus came and restored that garden of connection for you and me forever. Prayer is one of the greatest gifts Jesus gave us when he died on Calvary. Will you open the gift of prayer and discover all that is in His gift for you?

I pray that you will receive His gift of prayer and communion with Him today. From this day forward you will develop the Godly characteristic of prayer in a greater way than ever before. God bless you!

<u>Group Discussion Questions:</u>

1. What are some prayer models in this chapter that are new for you, or you would like to grow in? What are you most looking forward to as you grow in this area of prayer? Share and discuss.

   _____
   _____
   _____

2. Have you had any experiences in prayer when God revealed Himself to you in a way that touched your heart and life? Have you had a time when you realized He answered your prayer? Share your experience and encounter with the group.

   _____
   _____
   _____

3. Did those moments cause you to gain any new perspective on God, yourself, or your circumstances? Share with the group.

   _____
   _____
   _____

4. Did those moments cause you to desire more of the Godly characteristic of prayer in your life? If so, how did that start transforming you? Or how would you like to start transforming your prayer life? Share and discuss with the group.

   _____
   _____
   _____

5. Proverbs 20:12 *"Ears to hear and eyes to see-both are gifts from the Lord."* What is a unique way God has spoken to you personally? All of us struggle at times to hear the voice of

God. Share and discuss diverse ways He can speak to us and ask God to help you be open to hearing.

_____
_____
_____

6. Have you ever stepped out in faith to pray over someone else or have them pray over you? How did that impact you or them? If not, would you like to have that opportunity? Share and discuss.

_____
_____
_____

7. Take the opportunity to spend time praying for each other. Ask God to help you hear an encouraging word for someone else or to help you see them as He does. Share or pray what you hear or see. You can also write the prayer or encouragement down to give to them. We want this to be an uplifting experience, so only share what is encouraging. *"So now there is no condemnation for those who belong to Christ Jesus."* Romans 8:1

If you see or hear something negative, ask God what the opposite of that is, in its redeemed form, and release that. If you are unsure, then pray quietly to yourself for them. Filter what you hear or receive from others with Jesus and Holy Spirit on your own. What is from Him will draw you closer into a relationship with Him and you will have a deep peace and confidence that it is true.

_____
_____
_____

Homework:

1. Spend at least 15 minutes each day this week connecting with God in prayer. I encourage you to try a different prayer style each day. You might be surprised by the new way you enjoy praying and connecting with God.

   _____
   _____
   _____
   _____

2. Write down your experience each day so you can track and remember your process. Try not to pressure yourself that it must be amazing at first, or each time. This is just the beginning of a lifelong journey where you can start stretching out your wings of discovery.

   _____
   _____
   _____
   _____

3. Start your prayer time each day with Thanksgiving. Thank God for the Father, Son, and Holy Spirit for who they are and their role in your life. *"Enter His gates with Thanksgiving."* Psalm 100:4.

   _____
   _____
   _____
   _____

4. Get a special journal for Immanuel Prayer and try writing a love letter of gratitude and thanksgiving to your Father. Write on the top of the page, Dear Father God, I am so grateful for.... or Dear Father God, I remember the special time when.... And then write everything He speaks to you. Do not edit what you hear, just write.

_____
_____
_____
_____

5. Then flip the page over and write on the top of the page Father, what do you want me to know about what I have written? Pause, ask Him to speak to you, and wait. Then write.

_____
_____
_____
_____

6. Ask God to help you be open to Him and to allow you to pray for someone else that needs encouragement or healing. This could be in person, by phone, by text, or by video. Just try and be present with them in some way. Be wise if you are praying for a stranger to always make them feel honored and safe. Also, if they are the other sex, it would be wise to have someone else with you. You may also want to take the opportunity to go with someone else who has more experience in this or who you can encourage in the process. Write down your experience. Have fun on this adventure with God!

_____
_____
_____
_____

7. Quiet yourself in a secret place with Jesus and picture yourself at the foot of the cross. If you had a private moment to say something to Jesus as He was dying for your sins, what would you say to Him? Ask Jesus what He wants to say to you in that time? Ask Him how He sees you now under His blood? Ask Him how He sees you in the fullness of how He created you to be? Thank Him for all He gave for you to live

in your fullness. Ask Him to give you a word or vision of Him and you together in that place of fullness and joy. Write it down and keep it as a reminder and encouragement, especially on those challenging days.

___

Daily Prayer to Develop this Characteristic:

Father, I thank you for your precious daughter. You love her so much and you are excited for this new journey in your relationship through prayer with her. Help her to know your voice and to hear you loud and clear. Break off all lies of the enemy that would make her feel like she cannot hear your voice, or she is not worthy to receive. Release her from any doubt, fear, or condemnation and fill her with the joy of your presence. Help her to find new ways to connect and communicate with you in prayer and let it be special just for you and her. I pray she will be greatly encouraged and grow in intimacy with you, not only during this study but for the rest of her life. In Jesus' name. Amen

Journal Your Own Prayer:

Godly Characteristic #4
Obedience

Jesus said, "Those who truly love me are those who obey my commands. Whoever passionately loves me will be passionately loved by my Father. And I will passionately love you in return and will manifest my life within you."

John 14:21

Cathy Greer

Grace Church North County
Oceanside, CA
Mission Support Network
Kingdom Women Intl.
Founder and President

Cathy Greer is the founder along with her husband Stuart of Mission Support Network and currently serves as the President. She has served as a Pastor and is an ordained minister. She has trained many Pastors and leaders around the world. She desires to see the Kingdom of God advance through church planting, evangelistic outreach, and education for the poor. Cathy is an anointed speaker and moves powerfully in the prophetic and has spoken over many influential leaders impacting their lives.

She is an author and a mother in the faith of many forerunners and catalysts in this generation all around the world. She has a passion for seeing others walk in the fullness of their identity and inheritance in Christ. She is the author of "Welcome to Prophetic Ministry" and "A Quick Guide to Dream Interpretation." She is also one of the founders of Kingdom Women International. For more information go to www.msnministries.org and /or www.kingdomwomenintl.org.

Obedience

"Those who truly love me are those who obey my commands. Whoever passionately loves me will be passionately loved by my Father. And I will passionately love you in return and will manifest my life within you." John 14:21

When the phone rang, I was surprised to hear Tamara's voice on the other end. As if on an urgent mission she skipped the small talk and went into her purpose for calling. "I am authoring a book on the twelve attributes of Godly women. We are going to have twelve different women author one chapter representing the 12 Characteristics God had placed on my heart.", she said.

Honestly, I laughed thinking why are you calling me? If you know Tamara, you know she is surrounded by incredible women. Thinking about my intense schedule, I am chuckling at the notion that I would never have time for this. "What attribute do you want me to write on?" She responded, "I want you to write on the topic of obedience." Laughing I said, "I could write a book, not a chapter." I asked her "How are you going to do this?" Then she described a soaking, one-day writing retreat. As soon as I heard what she was attempting to do, I knew it was the Lord. God gave me a gentle nudge and told me, this is a gift to you, I am handing you something.

Tamara was being obedient to the voice of God; His vision and the result is a beautiful book and Bible study to impact the lives of every reader that encounters this book. Obedience always starts with God's voice and so I said yes to joining this study as a teacher and I will be obedient!

Webster's dictionary defines "obedience" as one who is obedient, submissive to the restraint or command of authority, and willing to obey. The New Testament word for obedience, *hupakoe*, is a compound word of two Greek words, *hupo*, "under," and *also*, "to hear." So, to obey is "to hear under."

I love how Bob Sorge defines obedience in his book "Secrets of The Secret Place." He states, "Obedience involves listening attentively with a heart of compliant submission and then, obeying God's word." The point is that obedience starts with listening. God speaks, we hear, and then obey. Of course, He speaks primarily through His Word, the Bible, but even as we study His Word, we tune into the still small voice, letting Him speak directly to us.

If you are going to listen and obey, then you are going to have to position yourself to hear His voice. That means we position ourselves to hear by reading our Bible, and spending time with Him developing our relationship with Him. Obedience always starts in a secret place with God.

For me, one of the most incredible examples in scripture of hearing God's voice and obeying, besides Christ himself, was Abraham. Reading His radical faith journey honestly brought me to tears. His dramatic story from leaving everything He was familiar with to travel to a place unknown and then the ultimate test of obedience, the sacrifice of His promised son Isaac starts in Genesis chapter 12 through chapter 25. I want to encourage you to read about this man who is not only mentioned in the Old Testament but the New Testament as our example of radical obedient faith.

How could one person walk in such radical obedience and faith? There is only one answer, He knew his God. He knew God was just, merciful, and could fulfill every promise. Obedience will always require trust.

I remember growing in love and trust with a man named Stuart, who at the time was my boyfriend. Our relationship was getting closer when he invited me to take a walk over to the park across the street from my house, I thought this is it, he is going to propose. The trees were so beautiful, the sky was blue, and the weather was perfect. Inside I was praising God for what was about to happen.

He finally stopped, turn towards me, looked me in the eyes, and said, "I need to ask you something." I thought to myself this is it! Then he said, "How do you feel about missions?" I quickly responded, "I love Mission Viejo," which was the city I was living in at the time. After he quickly explained what he was talking about, I was shocked and a little confused. I said, "No, no, no I can't do that."

Then I expressed my strong dislike of bugs. Except for a beach run to Mexico with my family as a kid, I had never left the country. It was a quiet walk home but, in the end, he still married me.

Married life with God and Stuart was nothing short of an adventure. He had already traveled to many nations and taken teams of people overseas to do simple things for the poor and encourage the church. Even my daughter went with a group of individuals abroad, but I had yet to go anywhere. Then one day, the senior Pastor of our local church, my boss, said he was going to Cambodia. Stuart actively encouraged me to go. I said I would pray about it. I did a very, very, short prayer and waited a few seconds. Hearing nothing, I told Stuart, "I didn't hear anything, maybe next time." That night I had a dream from God and when I woke up, I knew clearly that He was telling me to go on this trip.

It took me a few days, but I finally shared the dream with Stuart, and he said, "That's it! You are going to Cambodia!" Not only was the Lord asking me to go, but now my husband was telling me to go! I thought, "How can I get out of this?"

Immediate obedience was not on my radar. The closer we came to our departure, the more the fear began to mount. I knew if I was going to obey God, I had to do it afraid! Have you ever experienced the unknown and had to do it anyway? I would like to say I had the faith of Abraham, but I had the opposite, fear. I was not given any preparation or training for this short-term mission trip. All I had to prepare myself were the stories of the man we were going to meet in Cambodia, and they were not pleasant. His stories included persecution, jail, death, war, and the tragedy of the Cambodian people at the hands of the Khmer Rouge. To top it all off, I found out no one was going on this trip except the Pastor, his assistant, and me.

Finally, the day came, we were at the airport unloading the car when I broke down and started crying. I turned to Stuart and said, "Don't you love me? You're putting me on a plane with two men to another country!" He just laughed and said, "Honey, you're going to be ok, you're staying at a hotel. Plus, another couple is going to meet you there, don't worry."

He kissed me and handed me my ticket. I grabbed my carry-on luggage stood in line and watched him leave. I thought to myself, "That's it, he's gone and left me with these two men. He abandoned me, and I am going to Cambodia by myself. Why did I ever agree to this in the first place!" My thoughts quickly turned, "Are you sure you heard from

God?" As the plane loaded, I looked behind me for the nearest exit, but it was too late without making a scene.

I was finally on the plane and found my seat in coach while my boss and his assistant enjoyed the business class. I said to myself, "Yep, I am going alone, and now I am sitting alone." The fourteen hours of flying gave me plenty of time to imagine what lay ahead and it also gave me time to forgive my husband. As I was contemplating the worst, an unusual sensation come over me. I thought, "What is going on?" I had this awareness that everything was going to be good.

As the hours of flying continued, I felt better and better. Then something extraordinary started to happen. A supernatural peace flooded over me, and I became excited about my trip. Giggling to myself about my newly found disposition I looked up, and there was my boss. "Hey, how are you doing back here, Cathy?" He asked. "I'm good, I'm excited about our trip." As he walked back to his seat, I just laughed and thought, "This is crazy, a few short hours ago I was ready to leave my husband for putting me on this plane!"

In Genesis 12:1, we see God call Abraham saying, *"Go from your country, your people, and your Father's household to the land I will show you."* Abraham, by faith, gathered his family, belongings, and leaves. Can you imagine leaving the place you had known all your life, picking up your belongings, and taking your family to a place you knew nothing about?

It is easy to obey God when it is comfortable but when it is uncomfortable, what do you do? I had no idea why God would ask me to go to Cambodia, except the Great Commission in Matthew 28 says to "G*o and make disciples*". My favorite prayer at the time was, "Here I am God, send Stuart!" God did not just call Abraham for no reason; He gave him an incredible promise as well in Genesis 12:2-3. He said, *"I will make you into a great nation, and I will bless you; I will make your name great, and you will be a blessing. I will bless those who bless you, and whoever curses you I will curse, and all peoples on earth will be blessed through you."* What an incredible promise! I think that promise must have motivated Abraham for sure.

We also have promises from God as we obey His word. He said in John 14:21 that when we obey Him, He will reveal more of Himself to us. As we love Jesus through obedience, He also demonstrates His love increasingly to us and through us. Loving God through our obedience empowers us to obey Him even more. John 14:23 Jesus replied, *"Loving me empowers you to obey my word. And my Father will love you so deeply that we will come to you and make you our dwelling place."* Did you hear that? How many of you want to be a dwelling place for God? Come Holy Spirit! More obedience comes with the promise of more love and more power! Like Abraham as we journey with God, listen for His voice, and obey, we will also discover a faithful, trustworthy, powerful, and able Heavenly Father.

When I finally landed in Phnom Penh, gathered our luggage, and drove out of the airport into heavy traffic, I discovered the previously torn by war city, Phnom Penh was now an emerging city. So, you can imagine my shock when we arrived at our beautiful five-star Intercontinental Hotel. Before I knew it, I was on the 32nd-floor lounge sipping a cappuccino looking over this vast city. I thought, "Wow, if this is what Stuart had in mind on that walk so long ago, if *this* is mission work, then sign me up!"

Within minutes, leaders from the church arrived to talk with us. They were overly excited we had come to help them. Meanwhile, I was excited about my beautiful hotel room, and I thanked God for my vacation in Cambodia. I was so glad I said yes to God, as pitiful as it might have been.

The next morning, we went to the church to start the conference. I was curious about the Cambodian people, their culture, and their beliefs. They expressed to me their dreams and desires to go to school, find an excellent job and support their families. There were also orphans that lived on the church grounds. They were happy, eating well, and living in safety. These children had a chance at life that the kids I would soon meet in the city slums would never have.

Something was happening to me in Cambodia. Even my boss looked at me one day and said, "Cathy, you're not reacting like most people." I said, "Why, how am I supposed to be reacting?" He said, "I mean, you're not having any real culture shock. Even when we went and fed the people in the slums, you weren't depressed." To which I responded, "Oh, I didn't know I should be depressed, the slums were my favorite part of the entire trip." "Yeah, that's what I mean. That is not normal," He replied.

Before going to sleep that night I had a conversation with God, "What is happening to me? I loved the dirt and the slums. Lord, is there something wrong with me? Is this why you made me come here? To show me your compassion for the poor?" Yeah, I know what you may be thinking, "Aren't we Christians? Shouldn't we love the poor and the lost?" Yes, that is true. I am a Christian, but I am also an American.

I am from the comfortable, clean suburbs of California, remember I did not want to leave Mission Viejo. Seriously, I live in an area where they have valet parking at the shopping mall. Of course, I was reaching people in my community with the Gospel, and I was concerned about their spiritual destiny, but I did all that while making sure my Starbucks cappuccino was made with nonfat milk and had just a dash of cinnamon on top. Something different was happening to me here in Cambodia.

After wrestling with myself and my comfortable life, I finally drifted off to sleep. I was not out long before I was awakened. I sat up, wide awake and suddenly I heard a voice, "You're going to Africa." I was shocked and said to myself, "Oh no! I am losing it!" Then I had a thought, "Is this God?" I reasoned this could not be God I am in Cambodia, not Africa! Eventually, I was able to get myself back to sleep.

The next night similar things happened. After only a few hours of sleep, I sat up, wide awake hearing the same voice saying, "You're going to Africa." This time I got out of bed and said into the darkness, "God is that you? Why are you talking to me about Africa? I am in Cambodia!" I stood in the silence for a moment, then getting back into bed, I thought to myself, "Ok, this is crazy. This simply cannot be God. This is me we are talking about here; I'm terrified of bugs!"

As hard as I tried, I could not get back to sleep, so I decided to watch some television. Cambodian television. What was I thinking? As I flipped through the channels, I came across the only English-speaking station, National Geographic. Across the screen scrolled the word, "Africa." They were talking about a recent famine on the continent. I reached up and touched my face because it felt wet. I was completely unaware of the tears that had been streaming down as I watched this documentary. I turned off the television and forced myself back to sleep.

The next day was humid and extremely hot. We sweat through all the activities we had planned. We were so weary by the end of it all, that our dinner was short, and our goodnights were brief. After a quick shower, I crawled into bed thanking God for another successful day and I was out like a light.

For the third night in a row, I woke up and sat straight up in my bed. Once more hearing, "Go to Africa." I could no longer deny that it was God who was speaking to me, I got out of my bed, fell on my knees, and began to cry. As my tears soaked the carpet, I finally gave up and said, "Ok, I will go! Africa is a big place; I need you to guide me."

Wiping my eyes, I brushed the hair from my face. I breathed deeply and crawled back into bed. I had yet to discuss with anyone these nightly encounters, but I knew and there was never a doubt after them that I would be going to Africa. The question was more when, where, and how? The next day we were heading home.

Stuart was waiting for me at the airport. I was so happy to see Him. We loaded my luggage into the car, and I began to tell him about the trip. As we sat in the LA traffic, I excitedly told Him story after story. He finally interrupted me and said, "Where is my wife? Who are you?" I laughed, "I know, what happened to me, right? God did something in me." I did not tell him about the voice in the middle of the night, thinking it might be too much in one conversation. So, I waited to share with him about Africa. How was that ever going to happen? Still, I could not deny my encounter with the living God. James 1:22 says, *"But be doers of the word, and not hearers only, deceiving yourselves."* I wanted to do what God asked me to do, but how?

It was not long before I was back into my busy routine at the church when an email landed in my inbox. It was from an evangelist who was going to Africa and inviting others to go. This was it? Perhaps I should try to go? So, I talked to my boss about getting the time off. He was shocked that I wanted to go. I told him I would take vacation time, but I needed a pastoral reference to join the team. It was not a pleasant conversation, but in the end, he reluctantly agreed.

I headed home to talk to my husband thinking, "One down, one to go." By this time, I had told Stuart about my encounters in Cambodia regarding Africa, but he never said much about it. He is a practical guy. He only told me that if it were what God was calling me to, it would happen. I do not think he anticipated it would happen so soon.

Honestly, I was not sure of the timing of any of this but was simply trusting that many are the plans of men, but the Lord would guide my steps. I thought it might be wise to tell Stuart about the upcoming trip *after* he had enjoyed the wonderful dinner, I made him. He was more than surprised at my wanting us to go. I am sure he was thinking, "Is this the same woman I dated years ago? But doesn't she hate bugs? Now she intends for us to go to Africa?"

He listened patiently to all the details and then calmly concluded, "Let me think about it for a moment." Those few minutes felt like an eternity. Finally, he spoke up, "Where is this country located?" "Malawi, I think is west of Mozambique. We should look it up." I ran into the office sat at the computer and quickly found it on a map. Stuart walked in, took my seat at the computer began his research.

Thirty minutes later he came out and said, "I can't believe you want to go here." At that point, he did not think I was serious. Shaking his head in unbelief, He laughed, "Ok, let us see, it would cost us $6,000 to go plus another $1,000 to cover everything here while we're gone. If you can get the money, I'll go." I jumped up so excited, "Really? You'll go with me if I get the money?" He laughed, "*If* you get the money, I'll go."

The next day I shared with a few people that God had spoken to me, telling me to go to Africa and that I needed $7,000. People started coming up to me saying things like, "I heard you're going to Africa, here's a check towards your trip." Within a week I had $7,000. When I told Stuart that I had all the money we needed, he almost fell off his chair. He said, "I can't believe it, I only said yes thinking you would never get the money!" After a long silence, he sighed, "I guess we are going to Africa."

We did eventually go to Africa, but not to Malawi. Through a series of divine events, we ended up in Mozambique with the couple I had met in Cambodia. That first trip changed our lives forever and the next few years we were traveling to and from many nations in Africa. We were obedient to the call of God in our lives and because of it, we saw many miracles overseas and at home. What do I mean by miracles? People getting healed instantly, blind eyes seeing, deaf ears hearing.

This scared, comfortable Californian was now taking trips into remote villages, immersing herself in many diverse cultures and seeing the sick healed! We were learning life of being immediately obedient to God's voice whether that was going to the nations or our neighbors. We saw God move in powerful ways. As we hear His voice, read His Word, and obeyed His commands, we experienced His power manifest through our lives.

Sometimes waiting is obedience, and obedience is also action. We live in a world of so many voices that challenge God's voice. It is as old as the garden, "Did God really say?" Is there a promise, dream, or call in your life that is requiring a step of obedience on your part? If so, where do you need to trust God?

Sometimes we must rise and silence the competing voices around us and simply trust God. For me, each step of obedience leads to another step. I did not see the big picture when I took that first trip to Cambodia. I had no idea all these experiences over the years traveling were grooming me to make a significant jump into the nations.

We had already been greatly exposed to God's ability to provide in supernatural ways through our obedience. One woman paid for all my overseas trips for two years. That same woman came to me and said, "Cathy, God told me to set up a Nonprofit for you and Stuart because you are going to need it in the future." "What are you talking about, a Nonprofit? What would I do with it?" She said, "I am going to set it up, I think it's the Lord." So, we established a Nonprofit organization in 2005, called Mission Support Network, but we did not know what to do with it until three years later. We were waiting on God's timing. Which is also obedience.

Abraham had the promise that from God there would come a great nation and it would happen through Sarah. For Sarah, it was getting too long and so she reasoned her way into God's promise instead of simply waiting for Him to fulfill it. She took matters into their own hands. Their disobedience caused all kinds of problems resulting in the birth of Ishmael. You can read her story in Genesis 16.

Sometimes obedience looks like waiting. Waiting and trusting that the God who gave the promise can accomplish it. I wish I could say I cannot relate to Sarah but unfortunately, I can. There have been times in my life when I got tired of waiting and got ahead of God. If you are struggling in the waiting, seek God and get prayer. Command the fear that might be causing you to take matters into your own hands to leave in Jesus' name. In the waiting, get ready for the promise. What would that look like for you? Classes, learning a language, writing classes, speaking, recovery classes? Ask God, "Am I to simply wait or should I prepare for the promise and take a step?"

By this time, I was comfortable visiting the remote villages of Africa, but I always returned to a good-paying job, a beautiful place to live near the beach, and of course a Starbucks down the street. I had a passion and desire to go to other nations, but not to leave the comfort of everything I knew. My faith and obedience were about to be tested. Has your faith and obedience ever been tested?

For us, the moment finally came when the Lord said it is time to go, really go! Like Abraham, when God tested him by asking him to sacrifice his son Isaac, we were being tested. Would we leave the comfort of our Orange County life, secure jobs, and take the leap of faith into the nations? Would we give up the very things that we had loved and grown so accustomed to in obedience to His voice or would those very things around us become an idol, holding us back from our calling? Is there anything in your life that God is asking you to give up and let go of?

God began to speak so clearly and told us we were going to Ghana, Africa. We did not even know where Ghana was. Can you imagine this woman from Orange County, California was leaving for a place unknown and like Abraham, I had no idea what was going to happen, it was not easy, but we left, and God was faithful. That was eleven years ago, and we still have ongoing work in Ghana and have now traveled all over the world equipping pastors, and leaders, partnering in church planting, and are now building our third school in Ghana. We have seen thousands delivered, healed, and come to Christ.

> **Sometimes we must rise and silence the competing voices around us and simply trust God.**

In Genesis 22, *"Then God said, 'Take your son, your only son, whom you love— Isaac—and go to the region of Moriah. Sacrifice Him there*

"Early the next morning Abraham got up and loaded his donkey. He took with Him two of his servants and his son Isaac." Abraham was given *"as a burnt offering on a mountain I will show you,"* no explanation. He was just told to do it, plain and simple. *"Stay here with the donkey while I and the boy go over there. We will worship and then we will come back to you.* Notice that Abraham says "we" will come back to you after worshipping, meaning he *and* Isaac. Abraham believed the Lord would salvage the situation.

We see this faith displayed again when Isaac asks his dad where the lamb was: *"Abraham answered, 'God himself will provide the lamb for the burnt offering, my son."* Genesis 22:8

The altar got built but still no lamb. Now if I am Abraham, I am facing a crisis of belief. *Where is the help? Where is the provision? Where is the relief?* Not Abraham. He continues in obedience.

"He bound his son Isaac and laid Him on the altar, on top of the wood. Then he reached out his hand and took the knife to slay his son." Genesis 22:9–10. Of course, we know the story doesn't end there. God

interrupts: *"'Do not do anything to him. Now I know that you fear God because you have not withheld from me your son, your only son.' Abraham looked up and there in a thicket he saw a ram caught by its horns. He went over and took the ram and sacrificed it as a burnt offering instead of his son. So, Abraham called that place The Lord will provide."* Genesis 22:12–14.

God came through, just as Abraham had expected. Not only did God provide, but He also then rewarded Abraham's obedience. Abraham would have *"Descendants as numerous as the stars in the sky and as the sand on the seashore."* We are choosing to be obedient like Abraham and have seen many blessings. I want to pray for you and encourage you to live in the Godly characteristic of obedience and display to the world confidence like Abraham that you know who your Lord is and that He will provide everything you need for your mission.

God may not be asking you to sell everything and go into the nations, we all have our own personal journey with Him. Remember, obedience starts by simply hearing God and obeying His voice. Let me challenge you to walk in obedience today so that when we stand before God, we hear those beautiful words, "Well done my good and faithful servant."

Is there anything in your life that is a little *too* precious? Could you be making an idol out of something that God merely intended to be a gift in your life? Only you really know.

But understand, that God is always at work, molding and shaping us for His purposes. This sometimes comes through sacrifice, testing, and by trusting. When that happens, let Abraham's example be a blueprint for your obedience. And let the Lord's faithful sovereignty encourage you unto completion. We were created in God's image and obedience begins with hearing the voice of God. Listen intently and step out in faith because you will never know the road God has prepared for you if you never take that step of faith outward. God bless you and may you walk in obedience as a Godly woman for all the world to see.

Group Discussion Questions:

1. Has God asked you to do something? Has He asked you to put something on the altar and trust Him with it? How have you responded? Write and share with the group.

   _____
   _____

2. It is easy to obey God when it is comfortable but when it is uncomfortable, what do you do? Explain and share.

   _____
   _____
   _____

3. I asked myself that night in Cambodia "Are you sure you hear from God?" because I thought it was just too much, He was asking of me. How about you, are you sure you hear from God? Share an experience and how you are certain it is God.

   _____
   _____
   _____

4. Not only was the Lord asking me to go, but now my husband was telling me to go! I thought, "How can I get out of this?" Have you ever felt like that? Explain and share with the group.

   _____
   _____
   _____

5. My faith and obedience were about to be tested. Has your faith and obedience ever been tested? Share with the group.

   _____
   _____
   _____

6. Is there anything in your life that God is asking you to give up and let go of? Write it down and ask God to help you. Discuss it with the group and ask them to pray for supernatural strength and obedience. Discuss and pray with one another.

   _____
   _____
   _____

7. Is there anything in your life that is a little *too* precious? Could you be making an idol out of something that God merely intended to be a gift in your life?

Homework

1. True servants are found sitting at Jesus' feet "*Where I am, there My servant will be also,*" John 12:26 Sit at His feet today and listen to what He is asking you to do.

2. *"But be doers of the word, and not hearers only, deceiving yourselves"* James 1:22. Ask God if there is something He desires from you to do?

3. *"What He says to you, do it"* John 2:5. Ask God, for one thing, He would like you to do? Listen and do it. Write down what you heard and then pray about when, where, and how it will be done. Then wait for the Lord.

4. This week, every day spend 10 minutes asking God what is it TODAY that you want me to do? No matter how big or how small the assignment is, DO IT! This could be a simple phone call, gift, letter, or prayer for someone specific or He may give you a vision of a future call He has on your life. Write it down here and then be obedient as you develop God's characteristic of obedience.

Daily Prayer to Develop this Characteristic:

Father, if I have refused you in the past something you have asked me to do, please forgive me. Lord, make me brave. Lord, make me fearless. Father, give me the courage and the trust that I will do anything you ask me to do. I want to be obedient like Abraham and follow you to the ends of the Earth if you call me. God, watch over my movements and decisions and help guide me in the spirit of obedience. If there is a place you want me to go, or a job you want me to do, Father, I ask for strength to do it. I ask for eyes to see it. I ask for a mind to dream it. Father, I put my trust in you and know you are faithful and would never ask me to be obedient if it was to harm me. I love you Father, and I desire to do your will. Help develop the Godly characteristic of obedience in me through my everyday living and conversations with you. Thank you, Father, in advance for what you will ask of me. In Jesus' name. Amen.

Journal Your Own Prayer:

Godly Characteristic #5
Family First

The loving-kindness of the Lord is from everlasting-to-everlasting for those who (reverently) fear Him, and His righteousness to children's children, to those who honor and keep His covenant and remember to do His commandments (Imprinting His word on their hearts).

Psalms 103:17-18

Blanca Cisneros

Vineyard Church,
Anaheim CA
Free to Be Life Coaching
Founder, Coach

Blanca Cisneros was married thirty-five years to Robert and lives in Corona CA. In 2020, Robert went home to be with the Lord in Heaven. Together they have four beautiful children, four precious grandchildren, and three on their way. Through guidance from the Lord, Blanca home-schooled all four of their children 18 years.

Blanca was saved and committed her life to Jesus Christ when she was sixteen years old. She has served over forty years in various ministries including Sunday School teacher, Lay Counselor, Inner Healing Ministries, and has taught women's Bible studies throughout the years. Through the years she has been blessed to serve countless individuals, families, and youth, through teaching, mentoring, counseling, and coaching.

In early 2015, Blanca answered the call of God creating her new ministry FREETOBE and becoming a John Maxwell Certified Life Coach, RARE Leadership Coach and Trainer, and Biblical Counselor teaching and facilitating mastermind groups on personal growth development, character development, and the spiritual life skill of Emmanuel Prayer. She is passionate to help people who want to reach their potential by helping them gain insight and awareness of their personal growth. Equipping them with skills and encouraging them to explore areas in their lives where they may be stuck and empowering them to grow, gain freedom and transform to live a joyful life of abundance and be who they were created to be. For more info, www.freetobelifecoaching.com or email at blancafreetobe@mail.com.

Family First

Fear and panic gripped my heart, and I began to cry. It was a cold rainy day in December as the raindrops were pouring down on the window of my car. I was eight months pregnant with my firstborn and at that moment the realization hit me this baby is arriving in one month. I was sitting in my car sobbing at a Ross shopping center.

I prayed and cried out to the Lord; "Oh God I do not know how to be a mom!" I expressed my fear of not feeling equipped and not having a healthy model to follow.

The Lord said to me, "Remember how hard it was for you to speak because you felt you had no value and worth from being raised in your family?" I love how the Lord says, "remember then," He reminds me of a previous miracle He has done in my life.

Me: "Yes Lord, it was a five-year journey of your healing and restoring my brokenness from the pain of being raised in my family. Healing my identity in you, restoring my value and self-worth. Helping me have a voice, encouraging me to speak, that what I said did matter. It has been a miracle in my life!"

The Lord said, "I will help you and teach you how to be a mom. I will teach you how to love and care for your baby, and how to raise, teach, train, and discipline your child. Trust me, I will be with you!"

Me: "Thank you Lord because I know the miracle you did in healing my self-worth, restoring my value. Creating a new identity in who you said I am. I will trust you to help me be a mom." His presence and peace came upon me and with that promise, I took hold of His hand and entered this next season of my life, motherhood.

My journey of being a mom was about to begin. I was entering motherhood with no tools, or healthy models. In life, we tend to repeat what we saw our parents or family of origin model. Some of us had good role models and others may not have any or have dysfunctional examples.

Considering the family I grew up in, my journey of motherhood, family, and life is nothing short of miraculous; the way God transformed my heart and the next generation. My prayer for you in learning about God's *family first character* is to impart to you that no matter where you have been, no matter what you have learned, no matter what challenges you are facing now, there is hope. God can transform your family from brokenness to wholeness. God created the first family, and He desires our families to be healthy and strong.

When I was growing up, my home was not safe, it was a very violent atmosphere and I lived in fight or flight mode most of my life to survive.

My father struggled with alcoholism his entire life. He was violent, verbally, and physically abusive and caused much pain. I never felt safe with my father, I did not trust him, and we never got along. I also had two older brothers and they both were also verbally and physically abusive toward me growing up.

The trauma of our childhoods affected all of us and we took different paths. One brother got involved in a gang and ended up living a life in and out of prison and struggled with addictions. My other brother also battled a life of addiction to drugs and alcohol and lived a very isolated life. I also had a baby sister born many years younger and I loved her! My mother favored my baby sister which caused much pain for me, and I felt rejected and unloved.

It was difficult for my mother to live in a foreign country with no family and have a language barrier. As a result, my mother poured all her problems on me, she was controlling and manipulative towards me and depended on me to handle her affairs.

When my sister was a teenager, she felt abandoned when my mother divorced my father and moved back to Mexico, at which time I became my sister's legal guardian.

Being raised in my family I had much pain and brokenness in many areas of my life, but by the grace of God, I chose the path to become a Christian and seek a relationship with Jesus. Together, we did the work to heal my wounds, grow and mature in Christ, transform, gain freedom, and hope for a new future!

When I was twenty-five years of age, I married my husband, Robert. Soon after the honeymoon stage, the walls came crashing down, and our brokenness was exposed. He too was raised in an abusive environment. We both were raised in low joy family environments with dysfunction of every aspect of physical, emotional, and mental abuse and neglect. We individually entered the marriage with so much brokenness from our past upbringing and combined, our brokenness was magnified tenfold, and we were both desperate for healing.

The journey of healing and transformation has been a long, and sometimes complicated process in our marriage. My husband suffered from severe depression for many years of our marriage which caused much pain to me and my children. It also hurt Robert deeply as he struggled with guilt and shame for the damage that was caused and the pieces we would have to pick up. We have weathered many storms and have gone through many trials, but God is faithful and has helped us go through our deep pain and has taught us how to endure hardship well.

I can honestly say we have transformed, and I continue to see more growth, restoration, and redemption every day of God giving us back what had been stolen from us. It is a miracle we were married thirty-five years and were better in our end years together than we had ever been. If you find yourself in a difficult marriage or even just a broken soul from past pain, I want you to know there is hope and God is a God of miracles and restoration. I know how difficult it is to live in a dysfunctional family and pray God will speak to you through this week's reading and study.

God used our marriage to heal us. I thank God that Robert and I were both committed to our marriage and family; that our commitment kept us seeking God for healing and transformation. *"As iron sharpens iron, so one person sharpens another."* Proverbs 27:17. Robert and I sharpened each other to be our best selves, we made each other better.

From the beginning, we were committed to each other, to be honest, and learned to be kind with each other's weaknesses. We encouraged each other to learn and grow in the areas we wanted to develop. We challenged each other to become our best selves and through the years we transformed! We matured and learned how to live in love, joy, and peace with one another. Practicing joy exercises helped us become resilient in life and endure the hardships that life brought us. We became a better version of ourselves together becoming one.

From the very beginning, God valued families. *"The Lord God said, "It is not good for the man to be alone. I will make a helper suitable for him. Then the Lord God made a woman from the rib He had taken out of the man, and He brought her to the man." God instructed them to be fruitful and multiply, Eve gave birth to Cain, Abel, and Seth thus the first family was created by God."* Genesis 2:18, 22, 4:1-8, 4:25

There are no perfect families. Even the first family of Adam and Eve in the garden quickly were affected by sin. In the beginning, Eve was deceived by Satan and disobeyed God, you see Adam blaming the woman, then they both hid from God in shame. There was jealousy, anger, and murder amongst their children. Sin and dysfunction went hand in hand and from this day forward, we were forced to learn to battle temptation, sin, and seek restoration for our families.

God is love. He created us to have a loving relationship with Him and others. Why? Because God knows that if our relationship is right with Him and others, we can live in a joyful, peaceful state throughout life. *"God's greatest commandment is Love the Lord your God with all your heart, soul, mind, and strength. And the second is Love your neighbor as yourself."* Mark 12:30-31

As I have fallen more in love with God, it has developed a longing in my spirit which has made me faithful and obedient to seek God daily and throughout all circumstances for His perspective and truth. I have seen many miracles in myself, my marriage, and my family. God kept His promise and has been so good to me; guiding, directing, and helping me put my family first and in raising my children. We have four beautiful, wonderful children and four joyful grandchildren.

You might be saying to yourself, "I don't know where to begin to heal myself or my broken family," and I get it. I did not either. The truth is you cannot do it alone. It is only through the power of Jesus Christ that you can be healed, and the power of that healing transforms your family.

Let us look at where to begin. It truly begins with our priorities. Priorities are a fundamental starting point and so important to understand that those things that are your priority will get the focus of your time, talent, and treasure. In Matthew 6:21 and Luke 12:34 it says, *"For where your treasure is, there your heart will be also."* It is true! What is your priority? Our priority and intention must be focused on family first and then our heart will be committed to it.

When we are clear on our priorities and what we are committed to in our life, our thoughts and actions will follow. It will be the grid through which all your crucial decision-making will flow. You will filter everything that comes your way through that priority grid. For me, my priorities have always been God first, family second, ministry, and then business.

The Bible does not lay out a step-by-step order for family relationship priorities. However, we can look to the scriptures and find general principles for prioritizing our family relationships. God comes first: Deuteronomy 6.5, *"Love the LORD your God with all your heart and with all your soul and with all your strength."* All of one's heart, soul, and strength are to be committed to love God, making Him the priority with our time and adoration. He is your first love.

If you are married, your spouse comes next. *A married man is to love his wife as Christ loved the church."* (Ephesians 5:25) Christ's priority—after obeying and glorifying the Father—was the church. Here is an example a husband follows: God first, then his wife. *"In the same way, wives are to submit to their husbands as to the Lord."* Ephesians 5:22 The principle is that a woman's husband is second only to God in her priorities.

If husbands and wives are second only to God in our priorities, and since a *husband and wife are one flesh* (Ephesians 5:31), it stands to reason that the result of the marriage relationship—children—should be the next priority. Parents are to raise godly children who will be the next generation of those who love the Lord with all their hearts (Proverbs 22:6; Ephesians 6:4), showing once again that God comes first.

Deuteronomy 5:16 tells us, *"To honor our parents so that we may live long, and so things will go well with us."* No age limit is specified, which leads us to believe that if our parents are alive, we should honor them.

Of course, once a child reaches adulthood, he is no longer obligated to obey them. *"Children obey your parents,"* but there is no age limit to honoring them. We can conclude from this, those parents are next in the list of priorities after God, our spouses, and our children. After parents come to the rest of one's family. (1 Timothy 5:8)

My passion and priority in my life have been to first follow Jesus, seek Him and cultivate a relationship with Him, obey and trust Him, and allow Him to transform and grow me into His image. I am humbled by His tender care and personal involvement in my life, guiding and leading me to the abundant joyful, peaceful life He has for me.

My second passion and priority in my life have also been my family and children, to pass on the legacy of knowing Jesus as their Lord and Savior, that He is the way, the truth, and the life, and to cultivate a relationship with Jesus. Our priority is following God, and therefore our lives are working towards being a living example of helping our children grow in strong Christian values, morals, and character development.

> **Priorities are a fundamental starting point and so important to understand that those things that are your priority will get the focus of your time, talent, and treasure.**

Our example is far greater than anything we can verbally teach. The adage "Do as I say, not as I do" is not a great tool to teach because we know that our actions speak louder than words. Helping them to grow to be men and women of integrity, joyful, loving adults who add value and life to others has been my life's goal. Because I did not have these role models in my life, I sought out others who displayed Godly models and spent many hours in their presence, friendships and learned what I had not been taught so I could become the woman who God created me to be and reflect His character of family first. It begins in our homes.

This characteristic is not just about *your* family, but families' lives and we influence marriages, parents, and their children. When we can develop and encourage healthy families, we can become one of the greatest sources of discipleship and change our communities for Christ. People are looking for examples of Christ and it does not matter how much you impact the world if your home is a mess, you have missed the greatest ministry God has given to you. It is family first, and then you can go impact and influence others in your community and world.

My past affected my present. God showed me how my past affected my present. Personal and spiritual growth development entered my life and as I studied and gained understanding, it put a drive in me to take massive action to change the generational sin in my family's lineage. I wanted to impact and transform the next generation.

With God's help, I was intentional in making choices that helped me grow and change my mindset. I educated myself and implemented new tools to help me grow and transform which consequently helped equip me, my husband, and my children with life skills that promoted a healthy lifestyle. I was able to transform myself and change the generational dysfunction that was passed from generation to generation. The future would be different for my children and my children's children. We would be the point of change for this legacy of *family first*. Together with God's help and guidance, we have been able to help our future generations.

If you are desiring change too, you are in the right mindset. Change your priorities and commit to following God and His family plan first. God showed me I needed to heal and equip myself first. He showed me that it would be impossible to teach and give what I did not have myself so that is where I began. You cannot change people around you, but you can change yourself. Romans 12:2 *"Do not conform to the pattern of this world but be transformed by the renewing of your mind. Then you will be able to test and approve what God's will is— his good, pleasing, and perfect will."*

As wives, moms, and parents we need to ask God to illuminate areas in our lives that need to be exposed so we can grow in God's image and desire. God knows the areas we need to grow and develop to help us raise the next generation. *" Children are a gift from the Lord: they are a reward from Him."* Psalms 127:3

Here is a helpful guide I use in my life to prioritize my family and put them before other distractions of life. The acronym is BLESS. Let us break it down and keep it close as you navigate your way to developing family first Godly characteristics.

B - Be present
L - Listen and Lead by example.
E - Equip and Educate yourself with tools
S - Seek God and pray to gain insight and understanding
S – Share your God stories.

B - Be present, being present with your family is particularly important, time is one thing you do not get back so use your time wisely. *"You always have time for the things you put first"* as quoted by an unknown author. Ephesians 9:15-19 *"Be very careful, then, how you live —not as unwise but as wise, 16 making the most of every opportunity because the days are evil. Therefore, do not be foolish, but understand what the Lord's will is."*

I understand you may work, have careers, serve in ministries, or have other commitments, but I encourage you to take time and ask God for wisdom and direction as to who can help fill in the gaps. If you need help ask for help, you want to surround yourself with a joyful community of like-minded significant others like grandparents, healthy family members and friends, and childcare. Pray and then ask those that have your children's best interest and are willing to come alongside you and are willing to impart the love, joy, values, moral and character traits that are important to you.

Primarily, you as mom and your husband as dad need to be intentional to make time to prioritize and spend time with your family. If you are single, divorced or a widow, you have a more difficult job and need an even stronger circle of support and priority of time with your family, since you are doing the work of two parents.

I highly recommend you schedule it in your calendar. The key is prioritizing your family and spending time with them, and I encourage you to schedule and prioritize it just like any other appointment you put in your calendar, except I would encourage it to be the priority even before other activities are scheduled. This concept and activation plan will change your perspective and your actions will follow!

It is important to be present with your family, it shows them you love, care, value them, and are happy to be with them. It reflects the quality of family first and how God values us. You will begin to reflect on God's character and how much He loves us and desires to be with us first too. Everybody needs to know they matter, that someone cares, that they are valued, and that they belong. You can never go wrong cultivating a relationship with your family.

Investing the time in developing a relationship with your spouse and children is of excellent value and I encourage you to make it a priority. You cannot escape the consequences of one's actions. *"Do not be deceived; God cannot be mocked. A man reaps what He sows"* Galatians 6:7. It helped me to keep the end in mind, the importance of what I wanted to impart, cultivate and grow in my family and children.

When you set out to create and build a beautiful garden, you first begin by making a design, drawing in every detail to the plan including borders for boundaries, plants most compatible with weather and water, which need more sunlight than others. You choose the right soil and nutrients to feed your garden. It is much like your family plan for growth. Plant the seeds, water regularly, fertilize as needed, nourish them with tender love and care, prune off the old and dead branches and cultivate the harvest. The same principle applies with our family and children of keeping the end in mind helps us prioritize and stay focused on the goal of building the reflection of God in His beautiful family.

L - Listen and Lead by example. Listening is not always a natural skill one is born with, but it is a skill that can be learned. Learn to listen more and develop the skill of understanding the minds and hearts of your family when you are talking with them. Learn to ask more questions and then sit quietly listening intently. You will be surprised at how much more they want to share when they have someone who listens and cares. Be curious and ask questions so you can learn to understand what is important to them. James 1:19 *"My dear brothers and sisters, take note of this: Everyone should be quick to listen, slow to speak and slow to become angry."*

Clarify what you are hearing them say by repeating back to them that you have heard and ask them if this is correct. To become a good listener, you must develop the ability to connect and attune to someone else's emotions and feelings. It is important as a good listener and communicator that you validate their emotions. It is important to make eye contact by looking in their eyes and telling them you love them and that you hear what they are saying.

Lead by example. Your actions speak louder than words. Trust me it has taken me a lifetime to learn, practice, and cultivate this skill, and at times I still struggle, but I am aware, that awareness is the first step to change.

As parents, it is in our nature to be quick to give advice, but I encourage you to hold your tongue until they are done speaking. This simple, but unnatural skill is a game-changer in communication and relationships. Not only are we building trust and understanding, but we are simultaneously teaching our children how to communicate with the world.

We are empowering our children through our example of how to treat people and how to allow others to treat them. This is how we tangibly change the next generation with respect, kindness, love, and acceptance. Did you know that communication is 7% words, 38% voice tone, and 55% body language?

A word of caution; currently we live in a virtual world of smartphones, social media, and video games which means we are plugged in 24 hours a day 7 days a week. Full access, anywhere and anytime. What are you modeling to your children? If you are always looking at your screen, you are not present. Your children will do what you model.

I suggest if you work from home, it is important to have work hours. If you work away from home when you get home, I suggest having a basket by your front door so you can put your phone aside and unplug, shift your mind, and attention to your family. Unplug, and put your phones away out of your reach, especially at mealtimes. Family meals are a time for bonding, be intentional about putting electronics away including the TV during that time.

Do not miss opportunities with your family to learn about their struggles and victories. It could be a moment for them that will break their spirit or build their confidence. Today, we can be so busy with all the activities that we lose this opportunity to connect, and consequently, they will connect with others who may not be the best influencers. Be present, show you are happy to be with your family, and engage in joyful conversations. More youth and young adults are suffering from social anxiety because of the lack of relational skills. It is best to learn and develop relational and communication skills face to face. Your priorities will become their priorities.

E - Equip and Educate yourself with tools. With God's leading, I read the Bible, 2 Timothy 32:16-17 *"All Scripture is God-breathed and is useful for teaching, rebuking, correcting and training in righteousness,[7] so that the servant of God may be thoroughly equipped for every good work.",* encouraging books, attend personal growth workshops and marriage seminars to equip and educate myself with tools. This has been a way of life for me and was instrumental when I applied what I learned to my life that helped me grow and transform.

My husband and I would work on skills we were learning to improve ourselves and our relationship, and then we applied them to help equip and train our children. "The 5 Love Languages of Husbands and Wives" by Gary Chapman, was a terrific book where I learned my husband's love language and even began to understand my love language. I continued to read his children's series because it is important to know these languages as we communicate and affirm our family.

I also educated myself in understanding their learning style, so I could help teach and educate them with how they learned best, were they audio, visual, or kinesthetic learners. I learned about their personalities how they were wired, to understand their personalities, gain insight if they were introverted or extroverted, were more intuitive or sensing, were more feelers or thinkers. Each one was so unique, and I wanted to understand them to better equip each of them for life. I read God's word and taught my children Christian values and character development. Deuteronomy 11:19 *"Teach them to your children, talking about them when you sit at home and when you walk along the road, when you lie down and when you get up."*

S - Seek God and pray to gain insight and understanding. Seek God and pray for yourself, your husband, and your children. Teach your children to pray as well to cultivate a relationship with Jesus. Lead by example and model a life of prayer. *"Train up a child in the way He should go, and when He is old, He will not depart from it."* Proverbs 22:6

Seek the Lord. 1 Chronicles 16:11 *"Seek the LORD and His strength; seek His presence continually."* I set time aside to be in His presence, read the Bible, worship, use a journal, have conversational prayer with the Lord, and ask Him for insight, understanding, and guidance. Whether I need to grow and make changes within myself or if God wants me to make changes in my marriage or for my children; each child is different and unique. Do not put God in a box, He knows best! You are teaching and training your child in God's ways.

When my children were in their late teens, God showed me an area I needed to surrender to the Lord for Him to transform me. It was causing a wall between me and my children... my control issues. My control issues were causing division between me and my children and there was no peace in my household.

The Lord said, "You work so hard at controlling your children." The Lord said, "My motive to control those I loved around me was based on fear."

Me: I said, "Lord I want to keep them from experiencing pain."

The Lord said, "I saved you. I can save your children. Give your children back to me. Surrender this area of control in your life to me."

Me: "I give you back my children and I trust that you will care for them and save them as you have saved me. I surrender my children to you, and I surrender this area of my life, my control."

I came home and while our family was having dinner, I shared what the Lord had told me about my control issues. I confessed to them, and I asked for their forgiveness for me being so controlling and for the wall of division it was causing in our family. One by one they went around the table sharing with me how I controlled them and how it made them feel. I will share what one of my daughters said that broke my heart.

My daughter said, "I am happy for the insight you got from the Lord. The way you control me is, that you manipulate me with guilt (tears in her eyes). You try to make me do things by making me feel bad."

I acknowledged that this was true. I thanked her for sharing. I asked my daughter to forgive me. I committed to stop being controlling.

I committed to my family that day, I was going to work on my control issues, and I was going to stop controlling them. I said, "It has been a habit, and I am going to need your help to transform." I said, "I give you permission that if I fall and I am being controlled, please call me out on it because it has been a habit." As I worked on my control issues my children did call me on it when I fell into my old patterns of control. I would stop and acknowledge, you are right I did it again, I did not try to defend myself, I would say, "So sorry, forgive me, back to the drawing board." I kept working on myself.

Two years went by, and one day my daughters said, "Thank You!"

Me: I said, "Thank You for what?"

My daughters said, "Because you have kept your word. You have worked on your control issues and when we called you on it you did not try to defend yourself, you took ownership and kept working on it. You are not controlling anymore; you have transformed."

Me: I started to cry, it was the best praise report ever, I thanked them and told them I loved them.

My relationships with my family mattered so much and I wanted to cause peace in my home that I focused on connection. Keeping the relationship bigger than the problem, in your relationships with your family, spouse and children is key to living a joyful peaceful life.

It is important, to be honest, vulnerable, and transparent with your children. If you are wrong, the Bible says to confess our sins to one another (age-appropriate). We are not perfect and at times we may fall short, humble ourselves, confess and ask for forgiveness. *"Bear with each other and forgive one another if any of you has a grievance against someone. Forgive as the Lord forgave you."* Colossians 3:13

S – Share your God stories. I would share my God stories with my family. Share Jesus, communicate Jesus is relational and is alive and desires a relationship with your family and children. I shared openly my relationship with the Lord with my family. I shared my journey of life with them, I would share the life lessons God was teaching me and the outcome of the goodness and faithfulness of God in my life. Deuteronomy 7:9 *"Know therefore that the LORD your God is God; he is the faithful God, keeping his covenant of love to a thousand generations of those who love him and keep his commandments."*

The Bible is full of stories and God many times would say "remember." The prophets in the Bible would share their stories to the generations so that all knew the power and goodness of God. Share appreciation and gratitude stories with your children it helps grow joy in them. Teach them daily to share things they appreciate and are grateful for in their lives. This helps grow joyful children and families.

"Growth doesn't just happen; one has to be intentional" John Maxwell.

As I focused on keeping my family first, there were choices I made along my journey. God led me to homeschool my children, I homeschooled them for eighteen years. To help my family financially, I worked from home, I worked in the network marketing industry; I sold jewelry, then later health and wellness products. I had to schedule my time wisely between family time, teaching, working, extracurricular activities, sports, music, drama, (not all in the same season), date nights, and time with friends.

Raising children is a busy season and my encouragement and prayer for you are that you keep your family first. Seek God, pray, and ask God to help guide and direct your steps in keeping your family first. He will come alongside you and help you.

As I reflect and look back, my children are all now young adults. All my children are happily married, and one is in college. I am so thankful for God's faithfulness in helping me put my family first, guiding, directing, and helping us raise our children. They are grown people of integrity, strong Christian values, morals, and good character. They are joyful, loving adults who add value and life to others.

Our children's children are also reaping the benefits of the goodness of the Lord. God has helped us create a peaceful, joyful environment; our family loves to be together and we all love one another and get along great. We have fun and enjoy family gatherings. We come alongside each other when one is suffering and are tender with each other in our weakness.

At the time of this writing, my husband was suffering from Myelodysplastic Syndrome a bone marrow illness that affects his blood cells and was undergoing chemotherapy treatments. Our family was praying for a miracle of healing. Our children have all rallied around us to fill in the gaps and help where necessary. God is so good! I love my family! *"How good and pleasant it is when God's people live together in unity!"* Psalm 133:1. Unfortunately for us, God called Robert home, and we miss him terribly but know confidently he is home and God said to him, "Well done good and faithful child."

"A wife of noble character who can find. She is worth far more than rubies. Her husband has full confidence in her and lacks nothing of value. She brings Him good, not harm, all the days of her life. She sets about her work vigorously; her arms are strong for her tasks.

She makes linen garments and sells them; she is clothed with strength and dignity; she can laugh at the days to come. She speaks with wisdom, and faithful instruction is on her tongue. Her children arise and call her blessed; her husband also and He praises her." Proverbs 31:10-12, 17, 24, 25-26 and 28

Group Discussion Questions:

1. Take a moment and ask yourself, "What do I put first in my life?" Write those things and then discuss them with the group.

2. What are the things that keep you from keeping family first? Pray and ask God for wisdom and help. Share with the group.

3. Are you present when spending time with your family? Explain and share. Pray for one another to prioritize family.

4. On a scale of 0-10, How would you rate your listening skills? Discuss your answer and pray for increased skills.

5. Pray and ask the Lord to show you if there are any areas that you need to equip and educate yourself in to gain a better understanding? Write and share with the group.

6. Spend time in God's presence and ask Him if there is an area in your life that He would want to address in you or your family?

   _____
   _____
   _____

Homework:

1. Spend time in meditation and worship with the Lord and ask Him to reveal to you the priorities of your family. Write them down in order of priority.

   _____
   _____
   _____
   _____

2. Ask God to speak with you about the family priorities you are doing well and then praise Him. Write them down.

   _____
   _____
   _____
   _____

3. Then ask Him to speak more with you about those things that you could work on in your family that would help to cultivate a healthy family and minister deeply to your family.

   _____
   _____
   _____
   _____

4. Search the Bible for families that represent your priorities and list their names and characteristics that you would like to immolate in your family's first journey.

   _____
   _____
   _____

5. If you come from a dysfunctional family, pray about what has caused that dysfunction and write it down. Pray over it and ask God to restore to you what has been lost and eaten by the locust.

6. List out the names of your family members and create a special prayer for each one of them individually. Pray over them daily

Daily Prayer to Develop this Characteristic:

Dear God, the creator of the Heavens and Earth, you created a family with perfect design, and I thank you. Father, restore to me and my family the love and grace for one another. Help us to forgive one another and to walk in love and support every day of our lives. God, give me and my husband the wisdom and knowledge of family first mentality as we raise our children, grandchildren, and future generations. I thank you for your gift of family and Lord, I ask you to help me prioritize it and develop the Godly characteristic of family first. In Jesus' name. Amen.

Journal Your Own Prayer:

Godly Characteristic #6
Humility

If my people who are called by my name humble themselves and pray and seek My face and turn from their wicked ways, then I will hear from heaven and forgive their sin and heal their land.

2 Chronicles 7:14

Pam Booher

**Crossroad Church,
Corona CA**
Crossroads Church
Pastors wife and
Women's advisor

Pam Booher is known for her contagious joy, laughter, and passion for Jesus. Pam is married to her high school sweetheart, Chuck who is the Senior Pastor of Crossroads Christian Church in Corona, California where they both live. Pam and Chuck have been partners in ministry for over 40 years. Pam feels that Chuck is her favorite preacher and her best friend. Together they have two sons and five grandchildren. She loves Jesus and her church family who she pours herself into by leading the women's ministry, inspiring the photography ministry, caring for the staff wives, and being an encouragement to the next generation ministries.

Pam's favorite Bible passage is Ezekiel 36:26–27 *"Moreover, I will give you a new heart and put a new spirit within you; and I will remove the heart of stone from your flesh and give you a heart of flesh. I will put My Spirit within you and cause you to walk in My statutes, and you will be careful to observe My ordinances."*

For more information go to www.crossroadschurch.org.

Humility

One of my favorite quotes by C.S. Lewis is, "Humility is not thinking less of yourself, but thinking of yourself less."

In Romans 12:3, it says *"For by the grace given me I say to every one of you: Do not think of yourself more highly than you ought, but rather think of yourself with sober judgment, in accordance with the faith God has distributed to each of you."*

This verse is exactly what C.S. Lewis is saying. We do not need to put ourselves down and be a doormat, but we do need to think of others ahead of ourselves. We need to know who we are in Christ and be comfortable with who God created us to be. This is not an easy thing to do.

I have been married forty-one years to my favorite person on the planet who happens to be a Pastor. That makes me a Pastor's wife. You would think being Godly and doing the right thing would just come naturally to me, but I need Jesus in my life every day! I need to rely on Him for my attitude and actions. I want to be like Christ in all I do.

I know that humility is one of God's characteristics that He values for us as human beings. When we all practice humility, life would be so much better for everyone.

I remember when my second baby was born, I felt confident in how to nurse him. As I was getting set up to feed him for the first time, the nurse came in and told me I was doing it wrong, she scolded me, telling me I needed to lay down on one side and let him lay comfortably to let him suck from one side. I thought ok, I laid back down and got on one side and put him up against my breast, but he could not latch on, so I moved him in closer and I saw that I was smothering him. Poor little guy, he was drowning, and I was blocking his nose from breathing! It was awful! As a young mom I was still unsure of how to be a mom, thinking back to that nurse, her pride hurt me in ways I still remember thirty-five years later. I did not appreciate being scolded and feeling like my opinion did not matter.

Humility is not a popular thought or practice in today's culture. Sometimes, we feel as if we are entitled to many things that this world has to offer money, position, acclaim – and we do not have to work for it. Along with that, a feeling that "it just isn't fair." Life is not fair!

Life was not fair for Joseph. We find the story of Joseph in Genesis 37-50. He was his father Jacob's favorite son, and all his eleven brothers knew it. At seventeen, Jacob made Joseph, and only Joseph, a robe of many colors. Joseph also had two dreams that all his brothers bowed down to him. No wonder they hated him, can you imagine having your younger sibling have a special gift from your father, then have dreams where you will all bow down to him like a king? The brothers plotted and sold him into slavery and took his beautiful robe of many colors and dipped it in blood and mangled it. When they got home, they told their father that he was taken by an animal and is dead. Jacob was devastated.

Joseph was brought to Egypt and sold to Potipher, the captain of the guard. In Genesis 39:2 it says, "T*he Lord was with Joseph, and he became successful.*" He rose and was put in charge of all Potipher's household. Potipher's wife thought he was quite handsome and wanted him. One day she called him into her room and took a hold of his garment and tried to seduce him. Joseph ran out of there as fast as he could, as she held on to the garment and cried out that he tried to rape her.

Joseph did not defend himself and humbly accepted what the punishment was, Potipher threw him into prison. He had every right to fight for his life, but he chose to accept what was happening to him. Genesis 3:21 says once again, *"The Lord was with Joseph."* Once again, he rose to be put in charge of all the prisoners. Whatever he did, the Lord made it succeed.

One day the Chief Cupbearer and the Baker were thrown into prison by Pharaoh. Joseph was appointed to them. One night they both had a dream and Joseph interpreted the dreams for each of them, which came true for each of them. The Baker was killed, and the Cupbearer was freed. Joseph asked the Cupbearer to remember him when he was freed. He forgot all about Joseph.

If I were Joseph at this point, I think I would be so discouraged and think I deserve to be released. Entitled. He did nothing wrong. Yet, Joseph continued to be a prisoner with no complaining or fighting his way out. He was humbly accepting where God had him at that moment.

Two years later, Pharaoh had a dream and the Cupbearer remembered Joseph! He called Joseph up from the prison to interpret his dream. Joseph told Pharaoh that God can show him what the dream means. And God did. The dream said there would be seven good years with plenty and then seven years of famine. Joseph had a plan to be sure they would survive all fourteen years. Pharaoh put Joseph second in command, just below Pharaoh himself. Joseph was thirty years old when he was put into this position.

WOW! Imagine if Joseph had fought Potipher or demanded a hearing with whoever oversaw the prison to fight for his cause? Sometimes I want to fight to be heard, for life to be fair, entitled. God knew what Joseph had to go through to be prepared for the future. Joseph accepted each turn even if it was not fair. Joseph was a humble man.

Even when his brothers came to him begging for food during the famine, he gave grace and forgiveness. Genesis 50:20 *"You intended to harm me, but God intended it for good to accomplish what is now being done, the saving of many lives."*

At that moment, he did not flaunt that he had a dream when he was seventeen and all his brothers bowed down before him. Joseph was humble and knew God had him all along his journey.

On the other side of humility is pride. Pride is a problem for every one of us. We all struggle with wanting to exalt ourselves to make ourselves look good. We want to look our best on Instagram and Facebook and share only the good stuff. If we find ourselves comparing our lives with others, then posting to make us look better, it may be pride that is at work in our hearts. I struggled with pride when I first became a follower of Jesus, but I did not know it.

Prom night 1974, It was my sophomore year in high school when I met the "popular" boy. I was so excited when he asked me out and invited me to his church. I loved going with him. One day my mom told me I could not go with him to his church anymore. As time went on, he chose to spend more time with me and his relationship with God diminished. He began to pressure me sexually and I eventually gave in, and I got pregnant in my senior year of high school. I was devastated!

We needed to tell our parents. My dad called a family meeting, and everyone thought it was best for me to have an abortion. I had no idea what that was other than terminating a pregnancy. Both Chuck and I went into the clinic and talked with a counselor. She began to tell me that it was just a mass of tissue and that having an abortion is my best option since it was my senior year. She said that I had so many fun things to do and that having a baby would ruin my life. So, I chose to have an abortion.

Chuck dropped me and my mom off at the clinic. It was hard being there. I remember being cold, talking with other gals that were in there to get an abortion too. One gal, from Arizona, told me it was her third one. When it was my turn to go in, they told me I had to be put to sleep because I was thirteen weeks along.

When I woke up, I knew I had just done something wrong. VERY WRONG. As I lay there my heart hurt. I just wanted to go back in time. I could not take it back. It was done. I hurt deeply.

Chuck says that the girl he dropped off was not the same girl he picked up. I was broken. I was depressed. I did not care if I graduated. I did not want to participate in any of my senior activities. I even thought about suicide.

About four months later, I asked Chuck if we could find a church that we could get married in, not his or mine, but one that we could go to together. It was here that I first heard who Jesus was, that He loved me so much that He died on the cross for all my sins. Honestly, I knew I needed Him, I thought He would forgive everything BUT the abortion.

So, I gave my heart to Jesus and decided that I would bury having the abortion. I thought that is what God wanted me to do. I did not want anyone to know what I had done.

> On the other side of humility is pride. Pride is a problem for every one of us. We all struggle with wanting to exalt ourselves to make us look good.

It took about four years for transformation to take place in my heart and for me to fully receive the gift of forgiveness. We were married and in ministry when God began working on my heart. Chuck was in school to become a Pastor and he would come home and tell me the things he was learning in his classes. I loved it! Until he came home and said he was learning what an abortion was. He asked if I wanted to know. I told him, "No. At least not yet." God was stirring and I was getting curious. I began to ask questions of Chuck and what he was learning.

"What did they do in an abortion?" I asked. He began to tell me – the reason I was put to sleep was that the baby was too big to be scraped out through the tube. Oh, my heart was breaking, then I learned that they had to rip the arms and legs off him to suck it through the tube. Oh, my heart broke! I hurt deeply again.

I was learning fetal development during this time too and knew that the baby's heart is beating by six weeks. By twelve weeks the baby has his two hands and ten fingers, his two legs, and ten toes, and all his internal organs just need to mature to survive outside the womb.

I was heartsick. This was not a "mass of tissue." I cried for days. I asked God for help.

One afternoon our thirteen-year-old neighbor came over. She usually came over after school. She began to tell me that she had a new boyfriend and that she was thinking of having sex with him. My heart hurt for her. I wanted to scream. "NO. DON'T DO IT!" I know God was telling me to tell her my story. So, I did.

When I was done, she was shocked! She said she thought I did everything the right way because I was a Pastor's wife. WHAT? My heart broke. It was at this moment I realized I was hiding my abortion so people would not think bad of God, would not think bad of me. Pride. Oh, my heart was crushed. I did not want anyone to think I was perfect. I was the farthest thing from perfect!

It was that day that I prayed and asked for forgiveness. I knew God forgave me. I asked Chuck if I could share our story with our youth group. I had to humble myself to tell of the things that I had done wrong, to admit my sin. That was the beginning of my true freedom. I felt that the burden of hiding my sin was lifted off me the day I shared my story.

In 1 John 1:9 it says, *"If we confess our sins, He is faithful and just and will forgive us our sins and purify us from all unrighteousness."*

I was carrying a burden that God never intended for me to carry. God forgives! I needed to confess my sin, the abortion. Instead, I carried my sin of abortion around so no one would ever know. I did not let God work in all parts of my life because I was holding back a piece of it. He wanted to use my life as a testimony of His love and grace and forgiveness in my life. I realized that I needed Him more than ever as I went through this. Honestly, having everything out in the open, confessing my sin truly set me free. God was at work healing my heart. Humbling myself brought real healing and sharing my story has saved babies and brought healing to other women, and a few men.

Confessing our sin releases our pride so that God can work on us and in us.

In Luke 1, Mary was told by the Angel Gabriel that she would have a son. In verses 34 and 35, *"How will this be," Mary asked the angel, "since I am a virgin?" The angel answered, "The Holy Spirit will come on you, and the power of the Highest will overshadow you. So, the holy one to be born will be called the Son of God."*

Imagine what it was like for Mary to know she was being used by God to do something that culture told her was wrong. She knew that she could be killed for being pregnant and not married, yet that is how God chose for Jesus to come into this world. Her fiancé struggled with her pregnancy until God told him in a dream that it was, HE that did this! I cannot even imagine the pressure that was on Mary during those days, then to be a single mom. Oh my! Can you imagine that today? The pressure to abort would be great and overwhelming. And yet, Mary trusted God with her whole being. Her response was, *"Behold, I am the servant of the Lord; let it be to me according to your word."* Luke 1:38

I think about Mary often and how hard it must have been to walk with her head held high as a God follower and people not believing her. I thank God for her humility to say yes to God's plan for her life that could have cost her own life, but she trusted His way was better than the way of the world. I praise God for the strength that Mary had to walk through her life as a strong Godly woman.

It is NOT easy having humility every day! We are human. God knows this. Our greatest example of humility is Jesus, Himself. He left Heaven, a very safe place, to come to Earth and become a man just like us. We want to be like Jesus and these verses help us to keep our focus on being Christlike and striving to be humble.

"Do nothing from selfish ambition or conceit, but in humility count others more significant than yourselves. Let each of you look not only to your interests but also to the interests of others. Have this mind among yourselves, which is yours in Christ Jesus, who, though He was in the form of God, did not count equality with God a thing to be grasped, but emptied Himself, by taking the form of a servant, being

born in the likeness of men. And being found in human form, He humbled himself by becoming obedient to the point of death, even death on a cross." Philippians 2:3-8

"Do nothing from selfish ambition or conceit" I am constantly checking my motives to see if I am doing something to make me look good or to somehow benefit me. If I am, it is NOT from a Christlike heart.

"In humility count others more significant than yourselves." How do I view others... my husband? My coworkers? People at church?

"Let each of you look not only to your own interests but also to the interests of others." As a young mom, this one was so good for me to remember when my children were small. I never realized just how selfish I was until I had children. My eyes were opened! It was not easy dealing with my own selfishness. Plus, it does not say for me not to have interests, but to look at the interests of others, like our children.

"Have this mind among yourselves, which is yours in Christ Jesus, who, though He was in the form of God, did not count equality with God a thing to be grasped, but emptied Himself, by taking the form of a servant, being born in the likeness of men. And being found in human form, He humbled himself by becoming obedient to the point of death, even death on a cross."

Having this mindset helps us remember that God sent Jesus to be a man, to live here and be an example of how we can live as men, in a world that is out for themselves and prideful. Jesus became a servant, and not an equal with God.

My prayer for you as you finish this chapter is that you will be like Joseph, when a trial comes, you will know that God is with you every step of the way and that He will use you mightily when you are humble before Him and others.

Group Discussion Questions:

1. When was a time that you were prideful? Share what happened and how it affected others and yourself.
   _____
   _____

2. When was a time in your life that you had humility? Share what happened and how it affected you and others. Did they feel loved? Explain.

3. Think of people in your life that have displayed humility. How has this affected you? Share and discuss.

4. Think of prideful people you know, how had this affected you? Pray for these individuals and yourself.

5. Read the memory verse, 2 Chronicles 7:14, aloud. Write down and share what this verse means to you and our world.

6. What does this verse in 2 Chronicles tell us to do for God to hear us and forgive us? Share with one another and pray for each other.

7. Is it easy for you to accept where God has you in life right now? Why or why not?

8. Are there ways you can be more like Joseph? How?

9. Do you have a favorite Bible character that displays humility? How do they show humility? Discuss with your group.

Homework

1. Read the story of Joseph in Genesis 37 through 50.

2. What stands out to you? Write down your insights and wisdom to apply to your life. Ask God to help you.

3. Where would you struggle the greatest if you were Joseph? Does it affect your humility? How and why?

4. When life is not fair for you, what do you tend to do? Why? Pray and ask God to forgive you and help you grow.

5. Are there times when you KNOW that God is with you, and you choose to be humble with others and in your circumstances? Share with the group.

6. Have there been times that you chose not to be humble? What happened? Ask God to forgive you.

7. Do you have a list of verses that you can go to when you need help remembering to have humility?

8. Write out a verse every day this week on humility. Keep it with you to remind you daily. You can search humility, or humility in your favorite Bible app and find many scriptures to empower you.

9. What actions can you take today to help you remember to stay humble?

Daily Prayer to Develop this Characteristic:

Dear God, thank you for the amazing love you have for us. Father, forgive me if I have disrespected or dishonored you in any area of my life. Father, I ask that you remove all things of ego and self-righteousness in me and fill me up with your humility. Lord, I want to be like Jesus; gentle in spirit, full of love and compassion for others, thinking less of myself, and keeping a mindful eye to serve others. I am grateful that I can come to you and know that with your help and you in my life I truly can be transformed from selfish to selfless and prideful to humble. I thank you for your spirit that can change and transform me, gently correct me, and guide me on this journey of developing the Godly characteristic of humility. Thank you, Lord. In Jesus' name, Amen.

Journal Your Own Prayer:

Godly Characteristic #7

Servant Heart

*Just as the Son of Man did not come to be served,
but to serve, and to give His life as a ransom for many.*

Matthew 20:28

Nicole Forbes
The Rock Church World Outreach Center, San Bernardino CA
Youth Ministry Pastor

Pastor Nicole was raised in a Christian home but rededicated her life to Jesus twenty years ago. She has been married to Pastor Donny Forbes for twenty years and they have three boys, Nicholas, Seth, and Jeremiah, and a beautiful grandbaby. She graduated from The Rock School of Ministry in 2011. She served at the Rock San Bernardino in the youth ministry for nine years and Breaking Free for Youth Restoration Ministry for eight years, the past seven years, Pastor Nicole has assisted her husband in pastoring the youth and young adults, and the restoration ministry called Elevate Freedom at Elevate life Church in Riverside. Recently called back to her former Church to pastor youth at the Rock Church World Outreach Center.

She loves teaching Zumba and has been a Zumba instructor for eleven years. She loves helping women achieve their health goals spiritually and mentally. She has overcome with God's help and grace postpartum depression, self-hate, and lost sixty pounds. Through God's healing power, He has restored her self-image and their marriage. Her passion is to give hope to the hopeless, love those that are broken-hearted to life, and help them to see themselves as God sees them.

Servant Heart

As we begin this lesson on becoming a Godly woman with a servant's heart, let us begin with the definition of the word servant so we can clearly understand what kind of a heart we are seeking after as we build this Godly characteristic. The Webster dictionary describes "servant" as one that serves others; *especially* one that performs duties about the person or home of a master or personal employer; a person who is devoted to or guided by something.

My heart's desire is when you read this chapter of the book you would know what a heart of a servant truly is and what it is not. Being a servant of God is not just about doing good works, but it is about having the heart of your Father and being who God created you and me to be. To be a servant for God you need to receive His love and give it out to people around you by serving, performing duties, and being devoted to them, with our Father's heart and His love. Servanthood is rooted in love, especially modeling the love of Jesus.

It was a Sunday afternoon, and I was at my friend's baby shower. I was sitting around the table talking to my friends and suddenly, I heard my phone ring, and I heard my brother's nervous voice telling me that our father was in the hospital. My brother had no other details of our dad's condition. I was petrified by the news. I had prayed for two years that God would help me find my father since I had lost all contact and communication with my dad when he decided to go back on drugs.

I rushed to the hospital. I was so afraid of what I was going to find when I walked into his hospital room. All I knew was I had to get there. I said, "Please God do not let it be too late, do not let it be too late. I want to tell him that I love him, and I forgive him and ask him for forgiveness. Please do not let him die, God!"

In my heart that day, no matter what we have gone through in our past, our years together, or mostly apart, I wanted to be there for my father. I had told God in a letter I had written to my dad two years before; this was my heart's desire; I wrote, "Heavenly Father help me find my father. Lord, send me! I will help him! I will fight for him, and I will never give up on him! I will love him with your unfailing love."

When my friend Tamara Doss called me and asked me to be a part of her Bible study the *12 Characteristics of a Godly Woman*, I tried not to sound positive but that was easy because, to be honest, I was scared. I wanted to say no because I felt like I could not author a book let alone a chapter of a book. But before I could even say no, the Holy Spirit told me to say yes. Sometimes you cannot think about it you just have to be about your Father's business and when God speaks and tells you to do something, you just say yes and walk-in obedience. When we think too long about something, we tend to sit on it and get comfortable and not do what God is asking us to do. If He has called you, He has equipped you.

My friend Tamara said, "The characteristic I want you to write about is having a servant's heart." I was like, "What?" "Are you sure you want me to write about that topic because I am not going to the highways and byways? I am not on the mission field. I am not feeding the homeless." In my head, I thought that is what being a servant looked like. A servant was one out "serving" these populations day in and day out.

But I was wrong. Sitting here, I gathered my thoughts and asked the Holy Spirit to show me what a servant's heart looks like. He showed me an example with my biological father. See growing up I was daddy's little girl. I loved my father, but my mom and my dad got divorced when I was three years old. I did not know why but I felt the emptiness and void of that failed relationship. It haunted me for years.

All I knew is my life would never be the same and that is when I first recall feeling the spirit of insecurity, the spirit of fear came, the spirit of abandonment followed, and then the spirit of loneliness took root. That is the beginning of a little girl's life with a broken heart.

My mom filed for divorce because my dad was physically and verbally abusive to her. I see now why she had to file for divorce, but right or wrong, necessary, or not, the pain and hurt of not having my biological father in my life caused a deficit in my heart that I would have to battle most of my young life.

Growing up I always wondered why my father was not there for me, or my brothers and sister. When I was eleven years old, I learned and comprehended my father was a drug addict. I always wanted him to choose us more than the drugs, but unfortunately, that was not a choice he would make.

In the early days of dad's addiction, my heart remained faithful to my dad, and my desire to help my dad was still strong, but as time continued to pass by in my own life and he was not a part of my life it truly made my heart numb and hard. Eventually, I would not feel that pain any longer, I got used to it, and that part of my heart was hardened.

I remember praying as a little girl for my dad that God would help him and heal him from his addiction. I prayed that prayer for years. My dad would do well for a little while and then fall back into drugs. There was one time in my life that I thought he would not go back to drugs because he was clean for about four years, then he got out of his program and fell back into his habits.

It was disappointment after disappointment after disappointment. It got so bad, I confess that at one point, I just stopped believing in healing together for my dad. I had lost hope for a clean daddy to love me.

I had a dream about my dad. In my dream, my dad died alone on the streets. I woke up that night and I prayed to God "Please God, I do not want to get a phone call and find out that my dad died on the streets, and I was not there. Help me find him so I can be there for him, and I can walk out your Godly character of servant's heart and love him to life like Jesus loves us and gives us new life. God if you find him, I will be there for him, forgive him and serve him the way you have loved me and served me in my life." I did not realize what I was truly praying for, but God did.

Three years ago, God helped me find my dad. He was laying on a hospital bed and nearly died of a heart attack caused by a blockage in his main artery due to the forty-two years of continued drug use.

I remember getting that phone call at my friend's baby shower like it was yesterday, running out of the party and rushing to the hospital, crying out to Jesus about my deepest worries. I shouted out in panic "God, do not let me be late. Do not let me be late. Do not let him die. I want to tell my dad that I love him and that I forgive him and ask him to forgive me for having a hard heart against him."

I prayed that God would restore my relationship with my father. Are you wondering how all of this has anything to do with having a servant's heart? Truly having a servant's heart is not just going to the highways and byways and on the mission field, but your servanthood could be in your own backyard serving people you feel do not deserve it and have even hurt you.

It can sometimes be easier serving people you do not know because you are not expecting anything in return, but when you serve others that have hurt you over and over, that is exceedingly difficult to serve with a servant's heart. This kind of servant's heart is only found from supernatural unconditional love like Jesus at the cross. God is a God of healing and restoration. He wants to heal the broken places in our own hearts first so we can serve with the right heart, a heart with unconditional love. A love without conditions. That is a servant's heart.

Before we can live out the Great Commission, we first need to seek after God and develop this gift of unconditional love in our own lives. We need to "*Love the LORD our God with all our heart, with all our soul, with all our strength, and with all your mind, and love your neighbor as yourself.*" found in Luke 10:27. This is how we prepare our servant's heart. We must get right with God and have His heart to be a servant like Jesus. We also need to walk out our healing and restoration.

There is a story in the Bible that Jesus used in Matthew 25:33-40 that is a powerful example. It says *"And He will put the sheep on His right (the place of honor), and the goats on His left (the place of rejection).*

"Then the King will say to those on His right, 'Come, you blessed of My Father (you favored of God, appointed to eternal salvation), inherit the Kingdom prepared for you from the foundation of the world. For I was hungry, and you gave Me something to eat; I was thirsty, and you gave Me something to drink; I was a stranger, and you invited Me in; I was naked, and you clothed Me; I was sick, and you visited Me (with help and ministering care); I was in prison, and you came to Me (ignoring personal danger).' Then the righteous will answer Him, 'Lord, when did we see you hungry, and feed you, or thirsty, and give you something to drink? And when did we see you as a stranger, and invite you in, or naked, and clothe you? And when did we see you sick, or in prison, and come to you? The King will answer and say to them, 'I assure you and most solemnly say to you, to the extent that you did it for one of these brothers of mine, even the least of them, you did it for me."

Jesus wants us to serve people with His heart, with no discrimination. It is all about the lost and broken. By loving my father and being there for him in his brokenness, his addiction, his mess, I was serving Jesus because Jesus came for my dad. My father was broken, and God called me to love him and simply to serve my father with the heart of Jesus because that is what He did for me. Did I feel like he deserved it? Most of the time I did not think so, but God always reminded me, I did not deserve it either. He would remind me that He still chose to love me and serve me with His compassion even though I did not deserve it and I was still a sinner like my dad.

> **But God is a God of healing and restoration. He wants to heal the broken places in our hearts first so we can serve with the right heart.**

It is the goodness of God that draws men to repentance. (Romans 2:4) My dad needed mercy and mercy triumphs over judgment. (James 2:13) God wanted me to serve my dad with the unconditional love that His son Jesus gave to all of us. Jesus served us with His love and compassion when we were still sinners. He did not die for the righteous, but He died for the broken. John 3:16-17 *"For this is how God loved the world: He gave His one and only Son so that everyone who believes in Him will not perish but have eternal life. God sent His*

Son into the world not to judge the world, but to save the world through Him."

I love the example that Jesus displays to us with His twelve disciples in the book of John. We read in John 13:4-17. It is a beautiful picture of Jesus being a true servant. Let us think about this. The King of kings and the Lord of lords decide to kneel and humble Himself to wash His disciples' dirty feet. He washed all of them and He did not even exclude Judas that was going to betray Him a couple of hours later.

Jesus took a towel with which He girded His waste and put on an apron, by which Christ looked like a slave to whom the task of washing the feet of guests was assigned. Now would you wash each person's feet that came into your home daily? This was a custom they did in their culture.

The washing was a symbol of spiritual cleansing. Jesus always taught us spiritual things through the practical. Jesus washing the disciples' feet not only is a model of service, but it also represents the forgiveness of sins and wiping them away.

When my dad was in the hospital recovering from his heart attack and triple bypass surgery, his feet were so swollen and infected with fungus. He asked me, "Could you cut my toenails and massage my feet"? When He asked me my first reaction was, "No, I do not want to do it." I said, "Dad, you should ask the nurse to do it."

But the Holy Spirit spoke to me, and He reminded me of this verse in John 13:14-16 *"If I then, your Lord and Teacher, have washed your feet, you also ought to wash one another's feet. For I have given you an example, that you should do as I have done to you. Most assuredly, I say to you, a servant is not greater than His master; nor is He who is sent greater than He who sent Him. If you know these things, blessed are you if you do them."*

God spoke to me and said, "Nicole, don't miss this opportunity to serve me by washing your father's feet." God has given me a new revelation of being a servant. By washing my Earthly father's feet, I was symbolically washing my Heavenly Father's feet and was growing in the Godly characteristic of becoming a servant with God's heart for

His disciples. I got to serve my father in the last year of his life. Even though my father went back on drugs in his last year, and I was angry, yes, hurt, and disappointed, God would continue to remind me to serve my dad with love, compassion, mercy, and forgiveness.

When my dad took his last breath on this Earth, I got to hold my father's hand to his very last breath and moment of his life. It was a blessing to serve my father in the last two years of his life. God restored my relationship with my father because God gave me a servant's heart for the broken. Serving like Jesus requires not just sympathy for the brokenhearted, but empathy for them too.

"Empathy" is defined as the action of understanding, being aware of, being sensitive to, and vicariously experiencing the feelings, thoughts, and experiences of another. God will use the broken pieces in our hearts for His glory and allow us to get glimpses, or empathy, for others as we begin to love and serve with a true servant heart.

For us to display the Godly character of a servant, we naturally look at the characteristics and the life of Jesus. He is the perfect example of displaying the Father's heart on this Earth. In Matthew 20:26-28 it reads *"Not so with you. Instead, whoever wants to become great among you must be your servant, and whoever wants to be first must be your slave—just as the Son of Man did not come to be served, but to serve, and to give His life as a ransom for many."*

Verses 26 and 27 are talking about the measure of greatness is not position, power, or prestige; it is service. Jesus knew who He was. He did not have to try to be something He was not. His position on this Earth was to be a son first. When Jesus walked in His sonship, He was able to walk in servanthood and display a servant's heart on this earth with the right motives. In Luke 10:27 *He answered, "Love the Lord your God with all your heart and with all your soul and with all your strength and with all your mind; and 'Love your neighbor as yourself."*

There are many ways we can serve people around us. We can serve people with the love of God. You can serve them hope; you can serve them the truth; you can serve them food; you can serve them forgiveness; you can serve them mercy and grace; you can serve them by walking through a process of inner healing and restoration; you can serve them by a hug or a smile; you can serve your husband and children with love and compassion; you can serve in a ministry or you can serve on the mission field, but they all require a servant's heart if we are to truly serve like Jesus.

There are many ways we can serve our Lord Jesus, but servanthood comes from a heart of love. You must receive God's love in your hearts first or it will become a religious act. Let me explain. Many times, in our service we are busy doing good things, giving acts of service out to our families, in our crusades, with our time, talent or treasures, but without the heart of a Godly servant, they are a religious servant. God wants you to know Him and His love so that you can serve that love with your actions.

Food can fill an empty stomach, a roof can keep you dry from rain, and shoes on the soles of your feet can keep them comfortable and protected from the Earth, but only God's love can heal a man's soul. That is the key ingredient to a servant's heart and therefore serving man. Heal them with your love. Feed them with your love. Build for them with your love. Serve them in all that you do with God's love through you.

In any mission field, we find ourselves serving others, if we are not serving from a place of love, we will get bitter and disappointed when we do not get appreciated. I am not saying people will not take advantage of you and hurt you. That is a good possibility because hurt people tend to hurt people. But what keeps us from burning out, giving up, and saying, "I'm done!", but having endurance and pushing forward even when we get disappointed, discouraged, and hurt, is when we do it all from a place of His Love. Not your love, because our love has conditions, but His love is unconditional and sustains you.

We need to fall in love with our Father first and let His love transform our hearts. We need first to receive His love, so we can pour it out. If you have not received, you cannot give what you do not have. If you are running on empty, you cannot pour out. That is why it is so important to be with Abba Father daily and allow Him to fill you up with His unconditional love every day.

"As the Father loved Me, I also have loved you; abide in my love. If you keep my commandments, you will abide in my love, just as I have kept My Father's commandments and abide in His love. These things I have spoken to you, that my joy may remain in you, and that your joy may be full. This is my commandment, that you love one another as I have loved you." John 15:9-12

Your endurance is anchored in His love and that is how this will not become an "I have to do it" attitude, but it will come from a place of deep longing to love others because you realize and have experienced how much God has loved you and you cannot help but share it with everyone around you, even your enemies; the people that have hurt you.

Jesus did not discriminate, not with His disciples or others, even though He knew who was going to deny Him, who was going to betray Him, and who was going to nail Him to the cross. He still poured out His mighty love and sacrifice for all. *"Just as the son of man did not come to be served, but to serve, and to give life as a ransom for many."* Matthew 20:28

If we want to serve God with a genuine heart of faith, then we need to do it His way, by coming under His submission. What is the definition of "submission"? The dictionary explains it as the condition of being submissive, humble, or compliant. An act of submitting to the authority or control of another.

We see many examples of servants doing that throughout the Bible including Abraham, Moses, King David, prophets, disciples, Mary (Martha's sister), Mary Magdalene, and Jesus. All these people have a servant's heart of God. God's servants were those who worshiped Him and carried out His will. How did Jesus show us how to serve? By serving God through His obedience and reflecting His Father's heart on this Earth to the lost, hurting, and broken-hearted.

Many of us can do good works for the Kingdom of God but are they done with the right motives? A right heart? Are we serving God because it is the right thing to do? Or because we want to serve God by loving others? Jesus says in John 15 if we abide in Him, we will bear much fruit. *"Abide in Me, and I in you. As the branch cannot bear fruit of itself, unless it abides in the vine, neither can you, unless you abide in Me. I am the vine; you are the branches. He who abides in Me, and I in Him, bears much fruit; for without Me you can do nothing* "John 15:4-5

God's supernatural and unconditional love is the one who produces in us a servant heart because we abide in Him first. It is a heart transformation.

My prayer for you through this chapter and this week is to seek after the Lord and ask Him to grow your heart to serve others as His Son served us. I pray that you will always serve with gratitude, humility, and God's loving-kindness, generosity, mercy, and gentleness.

Group Discussion Questions:

1. What does the word servant heart mean to you? Write and share it with the group.

   _____
   _____
   _____

2. How do you see Jesus' servant heart? And what servant characteristics specifically do you see in Jesus that you want to develop in yourself? Why? Discuss it with your group.

   _____
   _____
   _____

3. Have you ever washed somebody's feet? Share with the group when and under what circumstances you were serving them? How did you feel as you served?

   _____
   _____
   _____

4. Pray and ask God for a list of people in your life He is calling you to serve? Family? Friends? People in the community? Write them down and pray over them frequently. Specifically, pray for God to reveal His love for them. Discuss and share.

5. When in your life have you ever been serving in the name of Jesus and realized you had the wrong heart? What made you aware of your wrong heart? How did you respond when you realized you were not serving with the heart of Jesus? Share.

Homework:

1. Spend time in the presence of the Lord this week and ask Him to reveal His servant heart to you. Write down all the aspects of a servant's heart He reveals to you.

2. Ask Jesus to lead you in the walk of developing this Godly characteristic of living life with a servant's heart.

3. Pray and ask Jesus to reveal to you circumstances in your past that you were serving, and it was for good works as opposed to serving with a heart of love. Write those times and circumstances down. Pray over them and ask God to change your heart.

4. Identify people in your life that need to be served and then ask Jesus which of these people, groups, or populations are the ones He is specifically asking you to serve. Pray and ask Him to give you the heart of Jesus for them.

_____
_____
_____
_____
_____

5. Sit with your Heavenly Father and ask Him if there is anyone in your life you need to ask for forgiveness. The way to serve most sincerely and compassionately is by releasing forgiveness upon them or of your own trespasses against them. Write the things He brings to your heart and mind. Pray over them frequently and be obedient in the act of forgiveness.

_____
_____
_____
_____
_____

Daily Prayer to Develop this Characteristic:

Father, I confess to you there are times I serve out of guilt or wanting to feel important, but God, today I surrender my life and time to you and ask that you give me a servant heart like yours. Fill me with your love and spirit to serve unconditionally, selflessly, without complaining or needing to be recognized. Lord, strip away anything that is not of your desires that resides in my heart and cleanse me fully of my sinful ways. God, restore me to the fullness of your goodness and sacrificial love for others. Thank you, Lord, for the work you have done in my life, and I desire to serve you boldly and compassionately wherever you will send me, but more than anything Father, I pray that you will send me a clean, pure servant heart and create in me a woman of God that everyone sees as genuine, sincere, selfless and reflecting your love in all that I do. God, I love you. Thank you for hearing my heart and I know you love me. In Jesus' name. Amen.

Journal Your Own Prayer:

Godly Characteristic #8

Honor & Respect

Give Honor, Esteem & Respect to whom Honor is due.

Romans 13:7

Roseanna Roman

Crosspoint Church, Chino
Founder of Morning Manna
Ministries Co-Founder of The
Christian Women's Word
Network & HSBN

Roseanna is the immensely proud wife of husband Danny, mother of Paul, who is now in Heaven, Tony, & Isaiah. She is a "Grammy" to 11-year-old Mellanie Jade & Baby Paul; Claudia is her daughter in love! Roseanna is currently an International Speaker, Conference Host, Author, Teacher, Preacher, Host of Morning Manna Tv Program, Director of Evangelism @ The Holy Spirit Broadcasting Network

Roseanna graduated from Long Beach State University in 1983 and was an elementary school teacher, graduated from Greater Love School of Ministry in 1989 and the School of Ministry in 2012. She was ordained in July 2017 as an Apostle & received her Honorary Doctorate from The Holy Spirit Broadcasting Network Apostolic School of Ministry under Apostle Andrew Bills, and authored a Prophetic Devotional, "Advancing in Adversity."

She has Founded the Kingdom Connection of women leaders, Unifying Impact Women's Conference, and Morning Manna Ministries. In 2017 Broadcaster on Morning Manna TV Program on the Holy Spirit Broadcasting Network, Co-Founder of Women's Word Network Tv Director of Evangelism at HSBN.TV

Honor & Respect

Nurturing a spirit of honor in my life has been one of the greatest blessings of my life! I believe that's why God has catapulted me out of the mundane into incredible living. Understanding this vital virtue principle will open the doors of blessing, opportunity, favor, unlock, and create massive doors of opportunity and preferential seasons in your life.

I have learned to cultivate a lifestyle of honor in enjoyable seasons of creating opportunities for others & intentionally recognizing and valuing others. I have learned to navigate honor in difficult seasons of dishonor, under cruel, dishonest, and disrespectful authority. I realized the greatest lesson of wisdom from God, "All authority is of God, but not all authority is Godly." In other words, God does not authorize ungodly behavior, but He does expect you to see beyond the behavior and honor the position of authority.

Understand ungodly behavior is not of God, but the position of authority is of God. Give honor to those who are currently in authority. Do not wait to give honor if they deserve it, give honor because they are already in positions of authority. "Honor" is a valuing of something weighty, precious, and costly. To honor is to, appreciate esteem, respect, notice, and favorably esteem. "Dishonor" is to not value, ignore, criticize, condemn, discount, or diminish.

David was a young man of honor, He continued to honor King Saul even though he persecuted him relentlessly. King Saul was a dishonorable ruler with a murderous spirit. David refused to dishonor a cruel, violent slanderous leader and God elevated him to the position of a King. Joseph was dishonored by his brothers, thrown into a pit, Potiphar's wife wrongly accused Joseph and Potiphar had him tossed into prison, yet Joseph remained honorable and rose to second in command in Egypt.

Moses was dishonored by Merriam and Aaron, they spoke against his leadership, and Moses remained a man of integrity and honor toward their disrespectful actions. He pleaded on Merriam's behalf not to strike her with leprosy. Moses was highly regarded and honored by God.

Jesus was dishonored, spit upon, nailed to a cross, abused, and battered, yet He prayed, "Father, forgive them for they do not know what they are doing." He forgave His enemies and died a painful death for sinners. He showed honor to ungodly authorities at the cross and how we are to honor and pray even for our enemies. Jesus was rewarded, given a name above every name that at the name of Jesus every knee will bow in Heaven and Earth. (I Samuel 19, Genesis 37, Numbers. 12, Philippians 2:9).

I experienced lengthy seasons of unjust mistreatment and dishonor. I have been persecuted and abused by Christian leaders and their flock. It was a painful, heart-wrenching time and there were many times I thought I would mentally break down and fall apart. My health was hit, and the heartaches were frequent and tremendous. Negative feelings of inadequacy, inferiority, worthlessness, and feeling I somehow was at fault for living out my calling.

This emotional turmoil was raging in my mind. There were times when my self-worth and self-esteem were being ripped and stripped from my very being. It was a tug of war with the enemy over my soul and my destiny was hanging in the balance. Satan is an identity thief. If he can steal your identity, he can steal and destroy your destiny!

The Holy Spirit continued to remind me that HE sent me on assignment to establish Morning Manna Ministry and teach believers that they can advance in adversity, progress in pain, and move forward in hardship (Isaiah 43:2). I was not to leave my place of assignment until the Holy Spirit released me. God did give me favor with the lead Pastors, and so I was able to build despite the oppression.

Have you been dishonored or despised by someone in your life? It hurts and can cause us to take a defensive or sometimes an offensive attack on them as we feel we need to fight back or even stand up for ourselves. From leadership, the spirit of disrespect, neglect, disdain, and scorn attacked my life vigorously on a grand scale, for reasons that are still unclear. I was never consulted, advised, or told why I was being dishonored.

God had called me to build a ministry for Him and so I remained honorable and respectful to all in authority whether they deserved to be honored or not. I knew God would not honor me if I engaged evil for evil.

God has instructed us to honor all those who are in authority, even when their behavior is ungodly. God promises us if we obey Him, He will reward us if we would commit ourselves to the living God and continue to do good. (1 Peter 4:19) The lover of my soul, the Holy Spirit was whispering "Don't return into a yoke of bondage and receive the spirit of rejection again, I healed you of that already."

He warned me "You will be mistreated, outcast, minimized, and devalued, but do not allow your heart to become tainted and poisoned with bitterness and resentment or you will disqualify yourself. Don't become angry and hostile or you will tie my hands from working on your behalf." He continued to say, "Make sure you do not take on the spirit of offense and withdraw from your place of assignment. I'm with you and I will elevate you above your mockers, scoffers, objectors, and oppressors if you obey me!"

> **Satan is an identity thief, if he can steal your identity, he can steal your destiny!**

I never thought any good could come forth from holding my tongue, keeping my cool, not returning evil for evil, not retaliating or reviling, not slandering or gossiping, not embracing a spirit of dishonor to become what I had been attacked by. I prayed for those who persecuted me, I confronted them with self-control and statements of gentle rebukes. I stayed under the control of the Holy Spirit and lived in honor. The Lord gave me a vision of me being elevated on the sanctuary stage if I would continue to stand in the place of calling. But the more they troubled me, the more I grew, the stronger I became, and the more wholly determined my spirit became to obey and walk in love towards my accusers!

As I did, seasons of reward began to pour over my life as the Lord elevated and honored my obedience in a dishonoring season. He elevated me on the very platform I was dishonored. My opposition witnessed the promotion, my naysayers heard of my elevation, my mockers viewed the honoring ceremony.

Morning Manna Ministry was given monies each month to run, we were given a staff to assist us to make Moring Manna a ministry of excellence. I was given an Honorary Doctorate Degree and ordained as an Apostle. My ministry was featured in magazines, I was on Tamara Doss's radio program, the Lord gave me my TV program on the Holy Spirit Network, speaking engagements started increasing, my first book was published, and I was given co-ownership of Christian Women's Word TV Network. Missions' trips are increasing to speak the word internationally and airfares are being paid in full!

I was promoted at the Holy Spirit Broadcasting Network as the Director of Evangelism. The Holy Spirit whispered again "Doors don't close to keep you out but to push you forward, when people don't accept you, you are not wrong for them, they are wrong for you!" The Holy Spirit is the spirit of truth, He said "You want local acceptance and I want global acceptance for you! I will take you from native lands to foreign lands." Seasons of reward follow seasons of honoring your authorities.

Honor Is a Spiritual Law

Spiritual laws have been set in motion by God and are just as sure as physical laws like gravity. Laws are keys that will unlock doors that have been closed because of a lack of knowledge, spiritual truths, and Biblical doctrine. Once you become aware of Biblical truth, meditate on the word day and night, confess the word, and live the word in your daily life, you will become a blessed and prosperous people. You will have wise dealings with success. (Joshua 1:8)

Honor is Wisdom.

Whomever you honor, recognize, esteem, elevate, appreciate, consider, and celebrate will be drawn to you. Whomever you dishonor, discredit, disrespect, dislike, reject, condemn, criticize, neglect, abandon and overlook will exit and step back from your life.

Joshua 1:8 tells us, *"Keep this book of the law always on your lips, meditate, on it day & night then you will be prosperous, successful!"*

Honor Has a Reward

Our Father, like most earthly fathers, desires to reward their children when they are following wise instruction with a pleasant attitude. Most parents will release a blessing, a reward, a prize, a benefit, a payment, a return for positive behavior. We need to realize after we have done the will of God in any situation, the gift of reward is on its way. Because your times are in His hand, so the blessings are timed-released into your life. God will reward you at the proper time and season. We need to renew our minds to expect to see the goodness of God in the land of the living, now in this life as well as in eternity.

Looking and longing for our blessing is scriptural, the righteous are rewarded with good. God rewards in this life. The righteous will be rewarded on Earth. In Galatians 6:9, We are encouraged *"not to grow weary in doing good, for at the right time a blessing will be released."*

Honor All Men Everywhere

Honor all men because all men were made in the image and likeness of God Almighty. Before you were placed in your mother's womb, He knew you, He planned for you, He created you, He gave you worth, value, acceptance, and approval before you were birthed upon the Earth.

Your value is God-given, unchangeable, unalterable, unmistakable, you are worthy of honor simply because of who you belong to and who created you. That fact will never change! You are already perfect, precious, expensive, worthy of honor! 1 Peter 2:17 says *"Show proper respect to everyone, love the family of believers!"*

A Hindrance to Honor

Possessing a spirit of competition will keep you from being honored by God and competition will keep you from honoring those that are due honor. Your flesh will not honor those that you perceive to be your rival. When you fail to honor and esteem others more highly than yourself, you halt the promotion God has prepared for you. It lets God know you are not ready to be elevated to your next level. Competition is fear of others passing you up, fear of loss, not being good enough, inadequate, less than, living in this state will stagnate and defile your Godly character and stunt your forward movement.

Jealousy and envy will cause you to depreciate and ignore those that should be honored because you feel threatened by their accomplishments. Having a jealous and envious spirit will cause you to be disqualified in the service of God, for He will not promote those who have tainted their anointing with envy. 2 Corinthians 10:12 tells us, *"He who compares and competes is not wise."* And Proverbs. 14:30 gives us wisdom, *"Envy rots the bones."*

Categories of Honor & Authority

God has set in place four areas of authority in our lives and honoring all levels will bring a Heavenly reward. These areas of honorable authority are civil, family, social, and church authority.

Civil authorities are presidents, police, and governments. These are God's servants. Family authority: husbands love your wives as Christ loved the Church, be a lead lover. Wives honor your husbands as a helpmate. Children obey your parents to receive the blessing of long healthy lives. The social authority of coaches, teachers, bosses, and employees are to be treated respectfully and fairly. Finally, Church authority. Honor those above you (pastors, elders, leaders, and teachers), besides you (peers), and under you (students, teams, and children). You will see flesh in these levels but honor anyway; obey and honor your leaders and submit under their authority for they keep watch over our lives.

Elders are worthy of double honor. (Ephesians 5:22-25, Exodus 20:12, Romans13:17, 1 Peter 2:17, 1 Timothy 5:17)

Group Discussion Questions:

1. Have you faced a time like David when someone did not like you and felt threatened by you? How did you manage it? Did you respond with honor, or did you give in to flesh?
   _____
   _____

2. How have you developed honoring authority in your life? Share with the group.

3. What circumstances in your life are you facing where you are being dishonored and/or disrespected? How can you respond like Jesus?

4. What Bible verses and promises to do you hold on to as you are developing the Godly characteristic of honor?

5. What emotions do you feel that rise in you that prevents you from responding honorably to authority? Ask God to help you respond like Jesus.

6. Take a moment to pray for one another in the group so you will be empowered to embrace honor as a Godly characteristic and to live it out as an example to the world.

Homework:

1. Take a moment to pray about someone in a position of authority you have responded to inappropriately and ask God to forgive you. Write it down and pray for them.

_____
_____
_____
_____
_____

2. Search out the story of David and read his story and how he responded to the King who wanted to kill him. What did God reveal to you in your own life?

_____
_____
_____
_____
_____

3. How did God bless David for his honoring of authority?

_____
_____
_____
_____

4. List out all the people in your life that you have contact with that are in positions of authority. Then pray for them that God will use them in powerful ways and that they are an example of honor themselves.

_____
_____
_____
_____
_____

5. Pray over yourself to honor each person from your list from question #4.

_____
_____
_____
_____
_____

Daily Prayer to Develop this Characteristic:

Create in me a pure heart oh God and renew an honoring spirit within me. I cannot do this life without you, and I cannot transform my hard heart into a heart of honor without your power and love. Father, please reveal yourself to me and help me to become an honoring and honorable woman of God in my life. I want to mature and think less and less of myself and increasingly like you and honor people like Jesus honored His Father. Thank you, thank you, thank you for what you have done for me by your sacrifice at the cross. You have given me everything and so Father I desire to give you everything. I want you to be glorified through my life and actions of honor and respect. Make me like you, increasingly each day. Help me learn what it means to abide in you and watch you produce blessings upon blessings in my life that I can share and serve others. Father God, give me glimpses of you and your glory today. I love you and thank you. In Jesus' name.

Journal Your Own Prayer:

Godly Characteristic #9
Faithfulness

I will sing of the mercies of the Lord forever; with my mouth, I will make known thy faithfulness to all generations.

Psalms 89:1-2

Peggy Stapleton
Sandals Church San Bernardino, CA
89.7 KSGN Christian Radio Business Development Account Executive, San Bernardino, CA

Peggy Stapleton is a Kingdom connector and has been a part of the 89.7 KSGN Christian radio station team for fifteen years. She is very Kingdom-minded and believes her role is to connect businesses and ministries to better serve each other as a community.

Peggy is a native Californian and is married to her wonderful husband Roger and together they have six amazing children, including their children's spouses. Peggy's first and most significant role is that of a mother, but most recently she has come to understand her newsiest and sweetest role of Grandmother of five beautiful grandbabies.

She served C.A.S.E. the Collation against Sexual Exploitation and C.A.D.E. Christians Actively Demolishing Exploitation. She also has served on boards of Hot Pink Warriors, Women World Changers, NAWBO, San Bernardino Community Church, The Non-Profit Network Association, Choices Pregnancy Centers, CASE Speakers Outreach, SBCC Women's Core Leadership, and The Barnabas Group Inland Empire and her home church of many years Sandal Church San Bernardino.

Faithfulness

My very first experience of God's faithfulness was listening to my mom share how she had waited ten years for her dream of children to finally arrive. She yearned to be a mother and after seven desperate years, her first baby was stillborn. She was devastated and heartbroken, not understanding why, but she continued to ask God for a baby. God was faithful and He answered her prayers three years later with three children. Her 10-year prayer had manifested and became a reality of living the life of motherhood she had always dreamed of.

I was the first-born child of those three babies birthed in a row. My two brothers followed me, and we were all born within three years. Wow! God is so good, and He is always revealing Himself to us in amazing ways. I never realized how important her story would impact my life. But as I write this today, I am honored to say I see the impact!

As she would always share how she waited ten years for us, my mother never failed to remind us of who was truly responsible for the gift of her children. She always glorified God and reminded us of His faithfulness. That deep faith and trust she had in God were being planted inside of me and it was a precious gift she gave me.

To this day, I am not even sure she knew the impact she had on my life with her faithfulness in prayer and trust in God. I have used the lessons of my mother's faithful story so many times to bring hope to others wondering if God is faithful. My story echoes my mother's trust in the Lord and that He is a faithful God.

Recently the word "reverberation" came out of my mouth as I was sharing an incredible story of a mother's profound impact on her sons who have been on a journey to reach a city for Jesus. This special city is my home city of San Bernardino, California. God had brought these two men to my city with the purpose and desire in their hearts to bring hope and love to hundreds of thousands of lost and hurting people that have found themselves in a very broken place. I kept hearing the word reverberation.

As I heard myself speak this word, I wondered to myself, "What did this word mean?" Was it even a word? I went to my phone and looked it up. "Reverberation" in the Webster dictionary means prolongation of a sound and echo; a continuing effect; a percussion.

WOW...A continuing effect. Isn't that the impact God's faithful story of love through His Son Jesus and the effect He has had on the world for generations? The faithfulness of God's great love for us is still having a continuing effect today.

What examples have you seen in your life that will echo and have a continual effect on the future generations of your family and your community? God calls us each to make a difference for someone through this life. We are all called out by God and have been given an assignment purposed just for us. *"God has prepared us in advance to do good works."* 2 Timothy 2:16

Maybe you are a mother, a sister, a wife, or a teacher. Whatever your role, you are a daughter of the highest King, and He will faithfully use you if you step out in faithfulness like my mother. If we, as faithful Godly women, can learn to trust Him in all circumstances; no matter what life brings us, we can make a difference for the Kingdom of God simply by our living example. Jesus was our living example in the Bible, and we have the assignment to be a living example to our family today.

We read about faithfulness and Jesus' example throughout the Bible, but we need to live that example to multiply the impact on those that need a real person facing real struggle as they watch how we handle our crises and trials of life.

I am excited to share a bit of my journey of God's faithfulness and I hope that you will be inspired to walk out your God-given design and purpose to leave a reverberation or lasting echo for generations to come.

Helen Keller once said, "Life is either a daring adventure or nothing at all." Let us come to recognize that we are on a God's adventure, and

He invited us to go with Him on this journey. What an interesting thought. In fact, for the last several years I have been on a bold God adventure, and sometimes it can be scary, but mostly it is exciting.

I did not know as I walked forward step by step, trial upon trial, failure upon failure, fear upon fear, what God would do with all the pieces of brokenness, challenges, and struggles that came along the way. I did, however, know that I have lived my life always asking God to teach me something in it all; the good, the bad, and the very painful and to never let any of it go to waste. Of course, He is faithful and so I have many lessons from my many struggles of life. I have learned unbelievably valuable lessons over and over and never let any of them go to waste. I have learned that faith triumphs in trouble.

Romans 5:5 says, *"Therefore I have been justified by faith we have peace with God through our Lord Jesus Christ through whom also we have access by faith into the grace into which we stand and rejoice in hope of the glory of God and not only that but we also glory in tribulation knowing that tribulation produces perseverance and perseverance produces character and character produces hope…now hope does not disappoint because the love of God has been poured out in our hearts by the Holy Spirit who was given for us."*

I got to see God's faithful character again in my own life. I pray you will ask God to reveal himself to you. I began my journey by simply asking the Holy Spirit to guide me step by step. This has been the most incredible journey as I chase the Holy Spirit from one divine appointment to another all toward sharing His faithfulness to help others see His plan in it all. Ask the Spirit of God to guide you and He will reveal amazing things to you.

If you have never asked the Spirit of God to lead you, then simply say "Spirit of God, I need you. I ask that you speak to me and share with me your ways. I want you in my life and I trust that you are my comforter and teacher. Thank you, Father, for your Spirit."

If you would have told me I would be sharing with you my story today, especially writing this lesson for you, I would never have believed you. I would have told you "Wrong." I would have told you "You are crazy!" You do not know me, so you would not know that I struggled in school. You see, I was the girl at the back of the classroom ready and happy to take an F on any paper I had to write just so I did not have to share with anyone. You find me today sharing with everyone in my city, echoing the goodness of God and the faithfulness of my mom and our God. I cannot stop sharing today and I pray I will remain faithful to God.

My life is like many of yours, a collage of beautiful stories, answered prayers, brokenness, stolen innocence, redemption, abandonment, love, lost love, hope, and a future. All our lives contain pieces of good and bad. It is only when the faithfulness of the God of the universe comes in and we allow the Holy Spirit to do His work in us do we get to see the picture unfold, God's fingerprints of faithfulness throughout the whole journey. I am getting a small glimpse of what that picture looks like on this journey. I believe with all my heart that God is redeeming everything I have been through in a bigger way than I could have ever dreamed.

In Proverb 3:5-6, we learn *"Trust in the Lord with all your heart and lean not on your own understanding in all ways acknowledge Him and He will make your paths straight."* That is His faithfulness in action. If you find yourself today in trouble and trials, take heart for God has overcome and He will make your paths straight.

I love people! Ask anyone I know. I am drawn to people and their stories. My daughters will tell you that I may be the only one they know that can go into a store and come out with a new friend and a lunch date. God wires each of us for our role and the purpose He has for us. The soul print, the cause within, is our DNA. "He *knew us before He formed us in our mother's womb,*" He tells Jeremiah "*I have set you apart as a prophet for the nations."* Jeremiah 1:5. He knows you too! And He knows me better than I knew myself. Our purpose has been planted within us before we took a placement in the womb. You cannot stop the plans of God.

As mothers, we can identify exceedingly early in our children their gifting and encourage and guide them to walk out their destiny. I am sure my mother recognized God's giftings in me long before I ever recognized them in myself. And if you have children, I am sure you see their strengths and value in this world. That is how God sees us. He sees, and knows, our strengths and value in this world. Your purposes are known to Him, and He is patiently waiting for you to seek Him, so you learn His faithfulness and learn to trust Him.

Ladies, I believed that I had identified my purpose early in life. My dream was to be a wife and mother more than anything in this world. I wanted to grow and build amazing kids. I can still remember at fifteen years old I found myself praying and asking the Lord not to come until that dream was fulfilled. Can any of you relate to that dream?

My youngest daughter just shared with me that she too had the same prayer in her heart. God did answer my prayer and I was living what I believed was my best life, an amazing husband, three incredible children, and a beautiful home. I was teaching Sunday School. We engaged in a prison ministry. It seemed that this perfect life would last forever but as with many of our stories, the path got broken and crooked. But through it all, it was God that remained the same, constant, and faithful.

CS Lewis once said, *"Hardships often prepare ordinary people for an extraordinary destiny."*

God took my broken story and used the still small voice of the Holy Spirit to make sense of the brokenness so I could remain faithful to what He was working out for a new season that was about to come.

Eventually, I would find a new job working at Terminix Pest Control. Can you believe that? A girl with a Godly plan and characteristic of faithfulness and God put me in a job where I would be killing bugs. Yikes! God has a sense of humor. I hate bugs! But God was teaching me to trust Him through this journey and provided an excellent job with provision to support my family.

Our family had just survived one of the hardest seasons of our lives when we found ourselves standing around the hospital bed of my first husband as he left this world for Heaven. The scripture *"life is but a vapor"* became a reality for our family. His life on Earth was over and it happened in real-time. He is now in Heaven, and we were heartbroken. Remember when I shared, "just because you are a believer does not exempt you from trials." It is true.

The Bible is a book of broken stories; Moses, Joseph, Daniel, David and so many more. They all lived through hardship, and it is the fire of those moments that refine and shape our trust in the Lord. God's faithfulness was what they and I held onto through the troubled times. I once again found myself holding onto Proverbs 3:5-6 *"Trust in the*

Lord." "Trust in the Lord." "Trust in the Lord." I knew He was faithful, and I knew I could trust Him.

A.W. Tozer once said, *"We can be in our day what heroes of faith were in their day but remember at the time they did not know they were heroes."*

In the fire was when I told God what I wanted to do. I wanted to go beyond just reading His word, I wanted to live it out. I wanted to use it all to be a force for good in the days and times He had assigned me here on Earth. You see it is no mistake that we are living in one of the most difficult and broken times in history. We have a front-row seat to see the scripture come to life on the nightly news. So many things contrary to God's word we are facing, and we are here to be His voice of hope, love, and restoration to His children.

There are so many testimonies of women in the Bible who have stood faithful to what God had called them to, even when it took great courage, courage even beyond their natural ability, but only by the spirit of God and their trust in the Lord. So many of their stories have encouraged me in my life journey. How about you? Does your life resemble a woman from the Bible? Mine does.

I think of Esther often and how God used her to save her people. We are all called to be Esther today. We must save our people. We have generations that have walked away from God and even those that have never been exposed. We must find our strength within and be bold about seeking God and knowing our purpose. Let us become a faithful women like Esther to save God's people.

Elizabeth trusted God for a son and got a precious gift late in life like my mother. How long do we have to remain faithful until God gives us the desires of our hearts? Are they God's desires? Are you willing to wait for God's timing? Until God prevails, we trust till the very end. We do not make our destinies; we wait and trust in God and His purposes for our life and then we will know that we fulfilled our destiny of being faithful to God and our purpose.

Mary, the mother of Jesus, was faithful through her experience of being a noticeably young unwed woman pregnant and yet had faith that God was using her to birth the Messiah. That is quite the responsibility for a young woman and yet through the embarrassment and challenge she faced, she believed what God had told her and she persevered through it all from pregnancy, motherhood, to watching her Son get crucified on the cross that fateful day, so we may live.

All these women of the Bible played an amazing role in the generations before us so we could know true freedom through their faithfulness to God, themselves, and what God had told them. Because of their faithfulness to answer the call to follow God, we have living examples to help us live our divine call and purpose too.

> There are so many testimonies of women in the Bible who have stood faithful to what God had called them to, even when it took great courage, courage even beyond their natural ability, but only by the spirit of God and their trust in the Lord.

Have you ever wondered if they were scared like we are at times? Scared to be faithful to that still small voice that whispers and calls us out into our destiny. God answered my prayer to make a difference and opened a door for me to walk through and that opportunity would change my journey forever. It made it possible for my purpose and calling to unfold to help others find hope.

A dear friend saw something in me that I did not see in myself, and she encouraged me to apply for a job at a Christian radio station, the same radio station we had listened to for years and that God used to encourage our family with daily. In 2007, I applied for a job at 89.7 KSGN, the largest independent Christian radio station in Southern California. Remember, God uses it all, even the wounds and scars. Will God find you faithful when you have healed but scars can still be seen?

God chose me for this mission because He had been planning and creating my journey for such a time as this. He created me with networking and connecting skills to help the Business Development Department. It came naturally, God-given. Remember, I love going to a grocery store and meeting new friends that were strangers only fifteen minutes earlier and having a lunch date? Gifts are used to connect people for purposes far greater than mine. It has been an incredible time over the years to watch Him unfold my skill sets to serve Him. These were the talents He formed me with that I did not see early in my life from hiding in the back of the classroom and not wanting anyone to see me, let alone hear from me. I would never have dreamt of the plans God had for my life. All I knew was a mom who was faithful and who taught me valuable lessons on God's faithfulness as she lived her life day in, day out. Faithfulness breeds faithfulness. Are you walking a faithful life and are people watching you live it? You never know who is watching, but you can change a life just by your confidence and trust in God's faithfulness.

So many good things were happening. He had placed a crown of beauty upon my head and gave me new opportunities from the ashes of my past hurts and failures like the promises found in Isaiah. One that comes to mind is a plane flight I took with friends over the Inland Empire. I did not know until that very day I would be flying and praying with six Pastors over the very area that our airways covered. We flew and prayed and anointed the land from the sky. You see, our part of the county had been hardest hit by the recession, so many had lost hope, so many had lost jobs, homes, businesses, and even many took their own lives through suicide. Hopelessness was all around us and, in the news, daily. But amidst the hopelessness, we found ourselves asking God to restore hope and reclaim the land with His faithfulness.

Crazy I know. It felt like one of the stories we have read about in the Bible. Being the only woman on the plane I prayed for women and children. I had my Esther moment. I was not going to back down with fear or feelings of unworthiness, instead, I seized the moment and led with faithfulness like Esther, Elizabeth, and Mary. Who but God could have connected all of us for such an important call to pray for our cities, and country, below on that fateful day?

My prayer as a young girl and my prayers as a grown woman was for this moment. My pest control experience, the one with bugs I despised so much was for this moment. You see the crazy thing was when I stepped into the airplane it all made sense. All the times I had to have courage as I worked at Terminix, conquering fears. It was all preparation for that very day. Only God could know what the future would hold and so He knew the preparation I would need.

In the plane were three brand new pest control sprayers filled with anointing oil. Coincidental? Of course not, all part of God's plan. I had worked in pest control and was the one who knew how to operate them. Only God could have authored this story. I have met so many women who have birthed new vision and ministry through this moment and experience of my life and I get so excited about what God did that day. I still see the reverberation across the Inland Empire in Southern California for generations ahead. I was so scared that day, but I knew there was a bigger purpose. So, I did it scared and that became my calling card. "DO IT SCARED!"

What is your life is God reminding you happened for His glory? Hold onto that story as I know God is going to use it to help someone in your path. His faithfulness is everlasting. His faithfulness has no time limits. Let Him re-ignite that fire that you thought was extinguished. Relight it. Trust in God. Ask Him to restore all that you have lost that you will need to be prepared for your journey to your destination. Embrace it all and *count it all as joy* as James would tell us.

Fifteen years have passed since the day I was hired at the radio station KSGN 89.7. He prepared my way and led me to a place I would serve my community connecting people and building bridges for so many amazing stories that have been written and will continue to be written. I learned that God could use my experiences to help others. I am honored to be a Kingdom connector and watch what His hands still create through obedience and faithfulness knowing He guides my purpose.

I have witnessed new homes for victims of human trafficking being built from nothing to reality by connecting women to use their journeys and their voices to help others. I have seen broken cities become renewed through the spirit of the Lord. I have seen churches be planted all over Southern California to bring hope to His people. I have seen hope connected across the nation and through hundreds of faithful people who believed in a faithful God. God's stories to share with you that I pray to encourage you to ask yourself these questions, "How do I become a faithful woman of God? How do I reflect my faithfulness to the world?" Once you have those questions answered, it's time to get busy executing God's plans.

We all have an opportunity to stand faithful where God has placed us. We are all created to be difference makers. We are all carriers of Jesus' story, and we need to echo His stories of faithfulness in our homes, to our cities and nation that will help transform lives, appointed by our Heavenly Father. What an incredible gift we have been entrusted with by our Father. Let us be faithful ladies to equip and encourage the next generation.

Life can change in an instant as so many of us have experienced. Not only can it change in ways we do not like, but it can also change in greater ways than we could ever imagine. When I started to chase the Holy Spirit with my whole heart and my whole life, I never knew what God could do. Was it risky? "Yes." Did I have to have courage? "Yes." But I knew God was the only thing that was truly faithful and stable.

God's love for me was the one thing I could count on in my life. I am talking about trusting Him in the dark days and trusting Him in the good days. I could rely on His faithfulness. He loves me and He loves you. Know this truth, *"Being confident of this, that He who began a good work in you will carry it on to completion until the day of Christ Jesus."* Philippians 1:6. God who started a good thing in you will be faithful to complete it.

I have watched the reverberation from my own journey in real-time. The echo rings out true and loud every day. I know on this side of Heaven I will never see what the impact will be on those I love and those that I do not really know, but I know someone is watching me. I continue to use my God-given skills and purpose faithfully to influence, connect with people, and watch what God does with my walk of faithfulness.

One thing I can count on is that my children and grandchildren will know that even when life gets crazy, God is always a safe place to run to. He is stable and never changing. MY GOOD, GOOD FATHER IS FAITHFUL.

I encourage you to walk in your destiny, your soul print, the purpose God has already written for you to influence a nation right where He has you planted. God authors your story better than you could ever write it, so seek His spirit, and listen intently to the voice of God as He directs your choices and decisions. Sit back, belt up, and hold on! He is going to use your faithfulness and knows He can trust you as much as you are trusting Him.

God is still answering my little girl's prayers, they just look a bit different. Now they look much fuller and so much richer than before as

He has redeemed the brokenness and straightened the crooked paths in my heart. I am living an incredible life with my wonderful husband, seven amazing kids, and five of the prettiest grandbabies you have ever seen along with a whole lot of wonderful women on the adventure of a lifetime, to impact the world for Jesus.

Are you ready to discover our faithful God? It is going to take courage and trust. You need Him so let us begin together to seek Him daily and pray for Him to develop your trust in His faithfulness and His good plans for your life.

Group Discussion Questions:

1. What examples and stories are you leaving for family and friends to trust the God that you trust?
   _____
   _____
   _____

2. What principles, values, morals are you firmly standing for in this world? Write them down and share them with the group.
   _____
   _____
   _____

3. Whose life will be impacted because you stayed faithful?
   _____
   _____
   _____

4. List three ways you have seen God's fingerprints and faithfulness in your life.
   _____
   _____
   _____

   Write in detail about the three things listed above in detail so you can pray daily and share them with others.

A.

B.

C.

Homework:

Search and study God's word. Then write down scriptures that will encourage you to remember God's faithfulness and help you to walk out your journey of faithfulness.

MY PROMISES OF FAITHFULNESS

1.

2.

3.

4.

5._____
_____
_____
_____

6._____
_____
_____
_____

Daily Prayer to Develop this Characteristic:

Father, I thank you for this day you have given me. I recognize that it is a gift of your faithfulness that I live and breathe the air in my lungs. You have been so faithful in my life and my family's life. I ask Father that you help me to become a Godly woman with the characteristic that resembles your faithfulness. Father, bring me circumstances and people that I can develop and reveal my knowing you are love and goodness. Father, search my heart and expose to me anything that is creating doubt or fear of the things of this world and help me to destroy those things and replace them with a faithful heart like Jesus. Help me to walk out of this life in faithfulness and help me to be bold and confident as I share about you and your faithfulness to your people. I love you and am blessed by you. Thank you, Father. In Jesus' name.

Journal Your Own Prayer:

_____
_____
_____
_____
_____
_____
_____
_____
_____
_____
_____

Godly Characteristic #10
Fruit of the Spirit

Thanks be to God for His indescribable gift!

2 Corinthians 9:15

Colleen Myers

**Springs of Life Church,
Running Springs CA**
PLUR Life Ministries Co-Founder, Director, and Chaplain

Colleen Myers is an Addictions Treatment Counselor and Chaplain who co-founded PLUR Life Ministries with her husband Rob of thirty-five years. She is a mother of three and a grateful Grammy of three. Colleen describes herself as a recovering judgmental church lady and loves to tell the story of how God broke her heart with the things that break His.

As the Operations Director for PLUR Life Ministries, she has gathered older moms, who she lovingly refers to as "The Menopostles," to minister to young adults at massive rave parties by sharing the good news of the Gospel, helping kids in trouble, and rescuing those in danger. These outreach teams of "rave moms" have interrupted human trafficking attempts outside of rave venues and assisted young people amid all kinds of dangerous situations. Since its beginning in Southern California in 2009, the ministry has grown to include outreaches across the country, and they offer a spiritual adventure weekend for follow-up at Camp 33.

Colleen is the author of Smack Dab - Living in the Center of God's Will, available on Amazon. For more information, visit their website at raveoutreach.com.

Fruit of the Spirit

A beautiful farm basket sits in my kitchen full of colorful, delicious-looking apples, lemons, and limes. I will never forget the first time my twin granddaughters noticed it when they were big enough and mobile enough to reach it. They each went for an apple. Their little hands grasped the fruit and brought it to their mouths. But one bite later, they simultaneously said, "Yuck!" and threw the apples like balls across the floor. The fruit looked great, but it was fake, and one bite told them everything they needed to know.

For years, I was like that fruit. I looked like a Christian, I talked like a Christian, but I was not living and walking by the Spirit. I had prayed for salvation as a child at Vacation Bible School and I did my best to be a good little girl. Today, I truly believe God in His great mercy saved me and that if I had died young, I would have spent eternity in Heaven. But as I got older, the truth was that my heart had not changed very much and those closest to me knew it. Like that fruit sitting in my kitchen, I looked good on the outside until life took a bite out of me, and then the truth came out. My fruit was fake.

Here is what that looked like. I was popular at my church. I led the women's group for a while, and then I took on children's ministries. I was a leader at my local MOPS group, I had volunteered at an orphanage in Mexico, I graduated from Bible college, I was a licensed Minister of the Gospel, I was a church secretary, I managed a Christian bookstore. I could go on and on listing all the Christian "stuff" I did and accomplished. But one day when our two oldest children were still little and our family was on the way to church, the truth came out.

My husband and I led worship at a church that was about twenty minutes from our home. As up-front leaders, it was important to me that our little family looked good on Sundays. The kids' clothes had to be clean and pressed and coordinated. The hairbows had to be just so, perched atop perfectly curled hair and the little jacket had to match the shoes, you know what I mean. My husband would wait patiently while I ran around like a crazed woman every Sunday morning doing things that he thought completely unnecessary.

We were late. A lot. Every single week, in fact. But so were many others who served at the church each Sunday. So, I was not too worried about it.

Then came the fateful elder's meeting where the staff was told that the tardiness must stop. They explained that it was not a sign of good leadership for all of us to be consistently late. Good leaders get there on time. Punctuality was stressed as quality of utmost importance. I grasped what they were saying and wholeheartedly agreed.

For the next couple of weeks, I was amazing! I laid out the kids' outfits the night before and got up extra early on Sunday mornings to be sure everything went smoothly. We could have it all and we could shine! My family could still look great, and we could also be great spiritual leaders at our church. I was proud that we had changed, but not only that, we were now the first people to arrive, ready to serve. If the elders were not there to see it, I made sure they knew that we were doing the right thing and I saw to it that they knew we had been on time, early in fact. It felt really good.

Then a few Sundays into this new way of life, something happened that threatened to ruin my newly acquired on-time reputation. About a year before, I had heard that an old friend of ours had made a whole lot of mistakes, started hanging with the wrong crowd, left his wife, and slipped back into old habits from his addiction years. A mutual friend had shared with us that Louis was using heroin again and it did not look good. No one had heard from him, and no one was sure where he was.

Well, that fateful Sunday morning I was proud once again to get everybody out the door and into the car on time, but there was a little glitch that cost us a couple of minutes. "NOOO!" I thought. We raced off to church, stressed but hopeful that we might still be able to make it, even though we might not be the first ones there. And then we saw Louis, standing on a corner, as we stopped for a red light.

My husband saw him first and pointed him out. He said, "Oh my gosh Colleen! Look! It's Louis. I think we should stop and talk to him. Maybe we can help."

My stomach immediately knotted up. Louis looked awful. He was half slumped over, and it looked like he had not had a change of clothes or a decent meal for days. It was a project that would take us hours to fix. We would be late for church. And just when we had fixed our reputation! We were leaders. Good leaders. That had to come first, didn't it?

I voiced all of this with a passion to my husband and when the light turned green, he reluctantly drove the car through the intersection and onto the freeway. The next week we got a call from our mutual friend. "Did you hear the news? They found Louis's body. He died of an overdose."

When life took a bite, my fruit was found to be fake. I was religion-led. I was people-led. I was not Spirit-led. God help me.

I have received forgiveness for what I did to Louis. I am trusting that the Father who loves us so much took Louis into his arms that day and he was finally free of addiction. I know for sure that Louis's salvation did not depend on whether I stopped to help him that morning. Even so, I wish I could forget that day, but I never will. Louis was finally free, but that day also marked freedom for me. Because on that day, my recovery from my addiction to religion began as well.

Without that day, and others that came after, where God used circumstances to break my heart with the things that break His heart (the foremost being my own sin), I would not be living out the call that God has placed on my life. Because He does not call religious people who do not think they need a Savior. He calls broken-hearted people who know what they have been saved from.

These days, when I introduce myself, I always start by saying, "My name is Colleen, and I am a recovering judgmental church lady." If you had been able to follow me around on that Sunday morning before I saw Louis for the last time on this Earth, and you'd had a minute to have a conversation with me as I rushed to get my kids ready for church, and if you had told me during that conversation that someday I'd be in full-time ministry to the lost and hurting of this generation, a certified Addictions Treatment Counselor, and a Chaplain who goes into prisons and emergency rooms to minister to young adults, I think I may have stopped curling my little girl's hair long enough to tell you that you were crazy and that I would never want anything to do with that kind of people.

But God!

Thanks be to God for His indescribable gift! Thank God that the result of that gift is the fruit of the Spirit in my life. It is an exciting way to live!

So, what does the real, honest-to-goodness fruit of the Spirit look like? The Bible uses this analogy of fruit to describe the work of the Holy Spirit in us and through us. Many of us are familiar with the famous passage found in Galatians chapter 5:22-23 that lists the fruit of the Spirit:

"But the Holy Spirit produces this kind of fruit in our lives: love, joy, peace, patience, kindness, goodness, faithfulness, gentleness, and self-control. There is no law against these things!"

Growing up, that list was so familiar to me that I had it memorized. Do not be too impressed. Since there are only nine fruits listed, it really was not that hard. Years of being in Sunday School and then years of teaching Sunday School had given me many opportunities to commit them to memory. I remember one of my childhood teachers displaying each characteristic on brightly colored paper fruit cutouts around the classroom. She earnestly begged us to work hard on showing each one of those fruits in our lives. And years later, when it was my turn to teach Sunday School, I earnestly taught the same thing, even though all my hard work had not paid off.

To me, those fruits were bullet points on a list; God's giant to-do list that I never ever would be able to accomplish. It was all so overwhelming. Of all the fruit, the first and the last on the list, love, and self-control, were the absolute hardest for me! Every time I saw that list, I would envision giant boxes next to each fruit that was to be checked off upon accomplishment. Why did the list have to start with love? I would never be able to get to the last eight fruits if I could not even check off the first one.

It was not until years and a broken heart later that it finally sunk in that this was not God's honey-do list for me to work on. It was His honey-done list for me, a list of blessings that God had already accomplished and had waiting for me and for those who would encounter Him, and all I had to do was be in His presence to experience every single one of them.

Perhaps you are new to this whole living in God's presence and walking by the Spirit thing. Or, perhaps you have felt that the fruit of the Spirit list is an overwhelming to-do list as I did. You have desperately tried to be gentle with your children, kind to your spouse, or patient with your boss. For the next few minutes, let us look at God's fruit basket with fresh eyes and see if we cannot peel away some old ways of looking at it.

In his letter to the Galatians, Paul uses the nine characteristics of love, joy, peace, patience, kindness, goodness, faithfulness, gentleness, and self-control to describe what will be in us and come out of us when the Holy Spirit is alive in us and when we are following His leading in every part of our lives. When Paul used the word "fruit" here, He was not referring to fruit as in apples and bananas. He is using a Greek word that is translated as "fruit" defined as "that which originates or comes from something; an effect; a result."

With that as background, I would like to suggest we define the fruit of the Spirit as "what comes naturally after the supernatural infilling and consequent indwelling of the Holy Spirit of Jesus in my life." Let's break that down.

The Bible says that when we are saved, His Holy Spirit comes to reside in us. As time goes on, we will know that has happened because we will become increasingly like Him and less and less like ourselves, as we once were. This process is called *sanctification* and it is a journey. As we settle into our new purpose in life, to glorify God and worship Him, we will see changes. For me it is simple: I sin less today than I did ten years ago, and I sin more today than I will ten years from now. That is just the way it is in the life of a Christian.

Paul describes the constant war that is going on inside every Christ-follower, and I love him for it! I am so grateful that he wrote these words that put him and every other Christian I know in real-life terms, and on level ground with each other. Because if we are truly honest with ourselves and with others, we agree with Paul's words in Romans 7:14-25:

"So, the trouble is not with the law, for it is spiritual and good. The trouble is with me, for I am all too human, a slave to sin. I do not really understand myself, for I want to do what is right, but I do not do it. Instead, I do what I hate. But if I know that what I am doing is wrong, this shows that I agree that the law is good. So, I am not the one doing wrong; it is sin living in me that does it."

"And I know that nothing good lives in me, that is, in my sinful nature. I want to do what is right, but I cannot. I want to do what is good, but I do not. I do not want to do what is wrong, but I do it anyway. But if I do what I do not want to do, I am not really the one doing wrong; it is sin living in me that does it. "

"I have discovered this principle of life – that when I want to do what is right, I inevitably do what is wrong. I love God's law with all my heart. But there is another power within me that is at war with my mind. This power makes me a slave to the sin that is still within me. Oh, what a miserable person I am! Who will free me from this life that is dominated by sin and death? Thank God! The answer is in Jesus Christ our Lord. So, you see how it is: In my mind, I want to obey God's law, but because of my sinful nature I am a slave to sin."

And there you have it, I was right. I will never be able to check off everything on that spiritual fruit list. And it is only by the grace of God that I will ever be able to have any of that fruit in my life. None of it can be manufactured by me because the fruit of the Spirit is made by the Spirit, not by the Christian. And the only way to get more of it is to get more of Jesus in your life. You can take all the anger management classes you want, sign up for every online self-help course you can find, practice yoga, learn deep breathing exercises, sing on the church worship team, go to seminary, and serve in your local soup kitchen every night, but none of that will change your heart.

A changed heart only comes through the sanctification process of getting closer and closer to Jesus by studying His Word, the Bible, and learning to hear His voice above all the others through prayer, where we talk to Him and then listen to what He has to say to us. A changed heart will come from remembering the good news of the Gospel every single day.

You will notice that I am not focusing on the fruit here. In this chapter, I am not going through each of the nine fruits and presenting definitions and research on each one and what they look like. For they all look like Jesus and so He will be our focus. I am focusing on His Spirit and what it means for Him to be a very real and active presence in our lives. The fruit is up to Him. That is His project, not ours. Thank God!

Let us look at someone who spent time with God. Let us see what fruit that produced in his life. This guy had a vision of being in the same room with God Himself! If that does not change you, I do not know what would! His name is Isaiah, and he wrote out his testimony of that experience for us to read. It is a white knuckler. When you get into it, you can hardly put it down.

In the beginning, the way Isaiah shares the Gospel is beautiful. In chapter 2:18, Isaiah writes out God's words that came to him in a vision: *"Come now, let's settle this," says the Lord. "Though your sins are like scarlet, I will make them white as snow. Though they are red like crimson, I will make them white as wool."*

Isaiah prophesies that God Himself would become the object of His own wrath in order to redeem us from it! How amazing is that!

Then in chapter 4, he shares that story of being in the same room as God. He says he saw the Lord sitting on a lofty throne and just the train of His robe filled the temple. That is some train! Isaiah describes all these angels around Him and how they were calling out to each other in words of praise to God and talking about how glorious He is.

Then it seems like a spiritual tennis match of sorts breaks out as God and Isaiah respond to each other.

And so, what was Isaiah's response when he saw all of this? Well, his whole perspective changed. You see, when he saw God in all His glory, he saw who he himself really was in comparison. And there was no comparison, not even close! So, Isaiah says, "It's all over! I'm doomed, for I am a sinful man!"

Then what was God's response? He forgives Isaiah of all his sin and removes his guilt.

Now the ball is back in Isaiah's court and here is what happens. In response to the incredible, unbelievable act of God's forgiveness of his sins, Isaiah says, "Here I am. Send me." Immediately, Isaiah wants to do God's will. That is spiritual fruit!

Here we are, way back in the Old Testament, and we see the Gospel and the Great Commission all in the book of Isaiah. God's heart is after the lost. When He saves us, He saves us from our sins, but He also saves us to serve Him and bring glory to His name by sharing the good news with others. That is His Great Commission to us.

When we are saved, we get a new perspective. Before, we thought we were all that and a bag of chips. We were in control of our lives. We created our own destiny. But when we see God as He is, and we see ourselves as we truly are, we get a new perspective. We gain God's perspective. And then He forgives us and washes us white as snow. We used to think God owed us something. We used to blame Him when things went wrong. Now we see the truth and we are grateful that things ever go right.

When we are truly saved, when God's spirit resides in us, we are so grateful for the Gospel, the good news of our salvation from sin, that our response will be like Isaiah's, "Here I am, send me. I want to do your will, God. Tell me where to go. Tell me what to say. Love through me." And that is when the fruit of the Spirit in us will begin to manifest and we will take joy in fulfilling the task that Jesus entrusted to us: to go therefore and make disciples of all nations, baptizing them in the name of the Father and of the Son and of the Holy Spirit.

If you are not seeing more and more of the fruit of the Spirit in your daily life, you must spend more time gazing at the Gospel. You must dwell on it, meditate on it. Do you remember what Jesus did for you on the cross? The Gospel is not just a starting point in your Christian life. You do not just hear the Gospel and then pray the sinner's prayer, get saved, and move on. The Gospel is at the center of everything you are as His new creation and it is the source of power to carry you from day to day, living and walking by the Spirit.

Ephesians chapter 4 talks about putting off and putting on. When you experience the Gospel, you are given a new nature, created to be like God. The Holy Spirit begins to renew your thoughts and attitudes. Increasingly you will put off your old nature and your former way of living and become more like Jesus.

"Since you have heard about Jesus and have learned the truth that comes from Him, throw off your old sinful nature and your former way of life, which is corrupted by lust and deception. Instead, let the Spirit renew your thoughts and attitudes. Put on your new nature, created to be like God – truly righteous and holy." Ephesians 4:21-24

> **When we are truly saved, when God's Spirit resides in us, we are so grateful for the Gospel, the good news of our salvation from sin, that our response will be like Isaiah's, "Here I am, send me. I want to do your will God. Tell me where to go. Tell me what to say. Love through me." And that is when the fruit of the Spirit in us will begin to manifest.**

Have you truly received the Gospel? Was it so long ago that you have forgotten? Maybe you got discouraged because you did not change as quickly as you thought you would. Maybe you got tired of the battle. Did you sit in Bible studies with other women and feel you did not measure up? As you looked around did you think you were the only one who had been abused, molested, neglected, abandoned? The only one who had ever had an abortion? The only one who had suffered a nasty divorce or who struggled with infertility, unwanted singleness, or same-sex attraction? Did you think you were the only one who had regrets and past sins that haunted you? Did you think you were the only one who cussed up a storm when things did not go your way? To cope with your perceived inadequacies, did you end up putting on the Christian face to try to save face?

God does not care about that Christian mask. He cares about your heart. And He wants to place His nail-scarred hands on every single place in your life that needs His healing, restorative touch. He wants you to experience the fruit of the Spirit in your life. Being the "only one" is a lie from the enemy. He wants to single you out. He wants to separate you from your sisters in Christ who can come alongside you and help you heal because they have been there too. You are never the only one.

Embrace this journey of sanctification and welcome others to join you along the way. Here is the key to having the fruit of the Spirit in your own life: Those who gaze into the Gospel every single day are those who have the fruit of the Spirit. Do you want to have that fruit? Gaze on and walk with and listen to the giver of that fruit. Look repeatedly at what God has done for you! Mull it over and over. Dream about it. Talk about it. Preach it to each other, not just to non-believers, but to your brothers and sisters in Christ. It should be a consistent story that we talk about repeatedly, incredulous at what Jesus has done for us! Only when we realize how much we have been loved and forgiven, can we absolutely love and forgive. Only when we grasp how much kindness has been given to us, can we truly be kind.

Do not buy into some of the modern-day teachings that the Bible is all about us. It is not. It is all about God. We are not the instigators, we are responders. We love only because He first loved us. He was running after us long before we ran after Him. He found us, not the other way around. We do not even have the faith on our own to believe, He gives us the faith. We do not manufacture the fruit of the Spirit, He produces it.

We must never forget that God loved us right where we were, right then, as is. In Romans, the Bible says that while we were yet sinners, Christ died for us. You did not have to clean up first. Need proof? Look at the thief on the cross next to Jesus. He did not have time to change his life. But Jesus saved him. Jesus loves you just like that thief! He did not love some future form of you. By grace He saved you. But it does not stop there, because that grace changes you! The Gospel changes you to LOVE as He loves, to have JOY that comes only because of that relationship that death on the cross allowed you to have with Him, to have PEACE that comes from the knowledge that you are safe forever, to have PATIENCE with others because of the patience He has with you, to show KINDNESS to others because He is so kind to you, to show GOODNESS to others because He has been so good to you, to show FAITHFULNESS as He is faithful, to be full of GENTLENESS because He is so gentle, and to exhibit SELF-

CONTROL because dying to yourself is nothing compared to God dying for you. And just like that run-on sentence I just wrote (it broke all the grammar rules, I know!), the fruit of the Spirit will run on and on and on in us and through us and all over everyone around us because the Gospel does not ever stop changing us.

If I have been gazing into the Gospel and thanking God for His indescribable gift of salvation that is just too wonderful for words, and someone cuts me off on the freeway, I am not going to flip him off and blurt out things about his mother or his backside.

If I have been gazing into the Gospel and thanking God for His indescribable gift of salvation that is just too wonderful for words, and my husband leaves for work with my car keys in his pocket, I am going to thank God that I even have a car. And I may even thank God that I have a husband!

The Gospel changes everything. It changes our perspective. If you do not see the fruit of the Spirit in your life, it is time to gaze at the Gospel again. New habits will form. It will become part of your spiritual DNA. Spending time in the same room as God will change you like it did Isaiah. As sanctification happens, your defaults will change. You will begin to default increasingly to love instead of hate, to joy instead of downheartedness, to peace instead of conflict, to patience instead of exasperation, to kindness instead of cruelty, to goodness instead of injury, to faithfulness instead of betrayal, to gentleness instead of brutality, to self-control instead of instability.

Ladies! Gazing into the Gospel has even removed the sting of others' sins against me! When I remember and celebrate the Good News of my salvation, I have a tough time being offended and holding others' sins against them. So much has been forgiven of me. I have even been able to forgive the abuse I experienced as a child because I see that it was the result of my abuser's sinful nature, inherent in all of us, and but for the grace of God, still controlling me.

Thanks be to God for this indescribable gift! It is too wonderful for words, and it fuels good works.

Group Discussion Questions:

1. When did you first realize that long before you were running after God, He was running after you? Share with the group.

   _____
   _____
   _____

2. What are some tangible ways that you can gaze into the Gospel every single day? Discuss with the group.

   _____
   _____
   _____

3. Do you have any "Isaiah moments" when you see how big God is? Share those moments with your group.

   _____
   _____
   _____

4. Did those moments cause you to gain any new perspective on yourself? How? Discuss in the group.

   _____
   _____
   _____

5. Did those moments cause you to say, "Here I am, send me?" If so, what happened?

   _____
   _____
   _____

6. What messages have been ingrained in you that keeps you from really believing that God could love you and forgive you? Discuss with the group.

   _____
   _____
   _____

7. Share a time that you felt fruit from the Holy Spirit being alive in you.

8. Even on your darkest, saddest day, what is one thing that you can be grateful for? Thank Him for that gift.

Homework:

1. For the next 5 mornings, set aside at least 10 minutes to meditate on the death and resurrection of Jesus and then spend some time thanking Him for His saving work in your life.

2. On the sixth morning, picture yourself at the foot of the cross. If you had a private moment to say something to Jesus as He was dying for your sins, what would you say to Him? Write it down and keep it in your Bible to read again on challenging days.

3. Notice the fruit that comes during the day from those morning moments spent with Him. Write down what God does in you and through you. Write down any changes you saw. Were you more patient, gentle, kind?

4. Turn to Romans 8:29-30. Write down all the verbs, each word that describes something God did. If the verb is mentioned more than once, write it down more than once. Then meditate on the list you have made and thank God for His work.

5. (This is like #4) Read Philippians 2:6-8. Then write down all the verbs you find in verses 7 and 8, each word that describes something God did. Then just like you did with the passage in Romans, thank God for His work.

6. Write a paragraph after reading Philippians 4:6-7 answering the question, "How can you apply this passage to your desire to have the fruit of the Spirit in your life?"

Daily Prayer to Develop this Characteristic:

Create in me a clean heart oh God and renew a right spirit within me. I cannot do this life without you. Please become bigger and bigger in my life. I want to become smaller and smaller. Thank you, thank you, thank you for what you have done for me on the cross, and in the tomb, and on that third day when you rose again. Make me like you, increasingly each day. Help me learn what it means to abide in you and watch you produce fruit through me. Please, God, give me glimpses of you and your glory today. I will be looking for you. In Jesus' name. Amen.

Journal Your Own Prayer:

Godly Characteristic #11

Hospitality

Above all, love each other deeply, because love covers a multitude of sins. Offer hospitality to one another without grumbling.

1 Peter 4:8-9

Heather Flores

Co-Lead Pastor at Elevate Life Church, Riverside CA
Founder of Embrace Women's Ministry

Heather Flores is Pastor at Elevate Life Church in Riverside, CA with her husband Tom of thirty-three years. She is the mother to three amazing young men and grandmother to her beautiful grandbabies. Heather is passionate about living out their church motto of "loving people to life." She is transparent about her past which includes drug and alcohol abuse, an eating disorder, and the heartbreak of abortion. She knows what it is to live for herself, and now feels honored to live for others.

In her journey following Christ, she has overcome what has been rightfully dubbed, "a religious spirit," and instead has learned to daily decide to love like Christ. They love to watch God go to work saving, healing, delivering, and restoring broken people just like themselves. They are certified marriage coaches, she founded Embrace Women's Conference showing all people hospitality, and that they are loved and valued; hosting the presence of God as He pours out His power and love on them, is one of her favorite things in life!

To contact Heather, go to www.elevatechurch.tv

Hospitality

Well, here I am writing to you about hospitality. To be honest, when I was first asked to write on this Godly characteristic, I did not feel it was a strong trait in my life. But as I prayed and sought God, I feel in many ways it is not only what I was created for, but what I love to do.

I guess when I first thought of hospitality, I pictured a beautiful woman in an exquisite home, wearing finely tailored clothes, with fine china and the most delectable hors d'oeuvres on a picture-perfect set table. Hospitality to me meant a woman who knows just how to arrange the table and stage the scene for an extravaganza.

Her home not only looks breathtaking, but it would also sound enchanting and smell aromatic. And those of us who do not share this gift are in awe, and secretly feel terribly inadequate compared to her. But the Lord began to minister truth to me, and I hope He speaks truth to you also through this week's Bible study with me as we unpack the Godly characteristic of hospitality.

If that which I described is your vision of hospitality, girl you have missed it! "Hospitality" is defined as the friendly and generous reception and entertainment of guests, visitors, or strangers; and anyone can do it. True hospitality begins in the heart, and we all have a heart.

The Lord whispered to me "Let all you do be motivated by love." You see the first description I gave of my understanding of hospitality really revolves around a "look at me" scenario and heart. This creates for many a feeling of "Oh my gosh! How do I ever aspire to that?"

But hospitality is based on the character and nature of our God, the author, and finisher of our faith, which is a characteristic of giving and sacrifice. True love involves sacrifice and love lives in one's heart. We must begin to understand that hospitality is a thought and feeling of serving others and making them feel loved and welcome. Hospitality is not about the hostess, but about the guests.

One of my favorite definitions of love is the sacrifice of self for the benefit of someone else. That is what Jesus did on the cross. *"For God so loved the world that He GAVE himself."* John 3:16. What the Lord began to minister to me, is that the Gospel, the "good news preached," is not about us but others. And true love and hospitality should never make others feel less than or inadequate but loved and valued.

I am a fan of beautiful and fragrant things along with scrumptious food, but the motivation behind its preparation is what makes the difference in the gift of hospitality.

I love the definition of JOY that we use to teach in children's church. Jesus first, yourself last, and others in between. When thinking about hospitality based on the word, God reminded me of Philippians 2:2-4. *"Then make my joy complete by being like-minded, having the same love, being one in spirit and of one mind. Do nothing out of selfish ambition or vain conceit. Rather, in humility value others above yourselves, not looking to your own interests but each of you to the interests of the others."*

The Lord immediately began to speak to me about love being the main ingredient in Godly hospitality. I believe if love is not the motivation behind ALL that we do then we have completely missed the opportunity to serve others well. The

But hospitality is based on the character and nature of our God, the author and finisher of our faith, which is a characteristic of giving and sacrifice. True love involves sacrifice and love lives in one's heart.

greatest commandment found in Mark 12:30 is to "L*ove the Lord your God with all your heart, soul and strength, and to love your neighbor as you love yourself."*

I believe when we genuinely love others, we will naturally show hospitality as God intended and extended to us. We will open the door, we will smile warmly, we will embrace our guests, and greet them with sounds of joyfulness as we serve and not be focusing strictly on the tasks or the physical beauty and perfection but be focused on the heart and desire of Jesus' love for us and others. We will set the atmosphere and show love through our every action. We will show love and honor through the gift of hospitality. And that love and honor are for everyone.

In James 2:2-3, we read *"Suppose a man comes into your meeting wearing a gold ring and fine clothes, and a poor man in filthy old clothes also comes in. If you show special attention to the man wearing fine clothes and say, "Here's a good seat for you," but say to the poor man, "you stand there" or "sit on the floor by my feet," have you not discriminated among yourselves and become judges with evil thoughts?"* Our God is not lacking any resources and I believe He has great pleasure in blessing His children as I do mine.

If love for people is our motivation for hospitality, I believe we will focus on trivial things as much as important things. That is why in our church I am into every little detail.

I like pretty things including fragrant soaps and flowers in the bathroom. It is clean and beautiful for every guest, so they are comfortable and cared for. In our lobby, it is decorated nicely, and we provide fresh pastries and coffee, and cucumber-infused water all as a gift for them. The staff and I discuss these things often and sometimes can have discussions about saving money or providing the best for our guests. I tell them I want the "good creamer," which of course costs more money, but it is a small detail that makes our guests feel loved.

I feel this way because I believe our church and the way we welcome God's children, not only represents the Lord but it shows people we believe they are important, and they deserve the best. Everything we do for the Lord, we desire to do with excellence and love, just as the Lord has given to us.

Can you imagine if people walked into the house of the Lord to see chipped paint and holes in the walls? Or carpets stained, floors discolored, or broken windows? Or dead flowers in the foyer and dirt laying around as though no one has prepared for them? None of the members of the church smile or greet them warmly? And there is nothing for them to eat or drink? No toilet paper or hand soap in the bathrooms?

Would we allow any of these things in our home, office, or church if the President or the Queen of England were coming to visit us? And if not, have we become judges with evil thoughts? How do you think that would make the broken person looking for hope and love walking into our church feel? What does that portray about our God? Our God is rich in provision and love. Our God who says *He owns the cattle on a thousand hills and is a good Father?* Our God loves people so much that He gave His very life for them. He gives us nothing but His best in love, thought, action and deed.

If our Father loves people so much, He was willing to sacrifice His only Son, and if Jesus values people so much He was willing to lay down His life for them, that warrants a response from us.

First, we love Him because He first loved us. And secondly, if God loves and values people this much, then we should too and those we serve should recognize it in us and feel our love and sacrifice for them at church, for a party, or at a simple dinner. We need to have an attitude of gratitude and servanthood.

If God would sacrifice so much to save us, deliver us, heal us, restore us, and bless us, we, in turn, would want to do the same for others. When we see people that do not yet know God's love, we should use every available means and opportunity to show them this great love. The Bible says, *"You will know they are my disciples by their love for one another."* John 13:35

One of the ways we do this is by showing love and honor through hospitality. I want people to feel they are valuable and that they are loved. Though it may sound silly, cleaning toilets, decorating the church, and providing snacks and coffee with good creamer is a quite simple, but important, way to do that and bring hospitality alive in our church. I find extraordinary joy even cleaning a toilet as I know it is showing love and service to God and His people. We hope to encourage everyone that hospitality involves everyone involved from the janitor to the greeter at the welcome center.

As I share about the importance of people feeling loved and honored in our church, the Lord reminds me of different experiences I have had at beauty Day Spas. Being a Pastor, I know that many people struggle with self-worth and self-esteem. Many people have deep soul wounds that affect how they see themselves. They see themselves in a light so vastly different than the way our Heavenly Father sees them.

My heart longs to see people understand who they are as sons and daughters of God; to help them know they are fearfully and wonderfully made by the creator of the Heavens and Earth, that they are valuable and amazing! So valuable Jesus died on the cross for them! There has been no higher price paid for a human soul.

If we can show people love through hospitality with kind words, smiles, hugs, and acts of caring, we can help heal some of their wounds as we love and value them the way Jesus loves and values them. So why during this writing did my mind travel to my Day Spa experiences? I think because of James 2:2-3 (above) and the act of humility and not judging people but serving all people with the same quantity and quality of value.

I have been to many different Day Spas over the years, and I have had quite different experiences at each of them. Every spa I have visited has been decorated beautifully and smells wonderful and sets the mood for a wonderful experience, however, that is not what makes or breaks the experience for me.

What does set the experience apart from others is if I feel loved and cared for; I feel valued and beautiful, my heart is warmed and I will likely return, and even bring others to experience the hospitality I felt.

However, if I walk into a Day Spa with a pompous atmosphere where every woman appears perfect and I get the feeling financial status is high on their spectrum of what is important, then I sense that I am not valued and I draw back. Whether my feelings are valid or not; if I feel less than, unimportant, insecure then I am out! I am uncomfortable and so I retreat or do not experience the beauty and love that I was anticipating and hoping for, just like seeking hope for Christ's love and acceptance.

Maybe it is just me. Or maybe there are a few other women out there that might feel just like me. Maybe I need some healing, but I feel slightly hurt and walk out of places like that. Our hearts must be right when serving in a role of hospitality at home or church. Every guest matters and they should know it.

I have never been comfortable in super high-end places, whether it be a clothing store or a restaurant, and I have never totally understood why. I grew up in an upper-middle-class in golf course community, and my parent's closest friends were rich. I grew up traveling the world and had my college education paid for even before I decided what university I would attend. So why is it I feel this way?

I guess because I know not everyone would be warmly welcomed there and my heart is filled with the Godly characteristic of hospitality. I want everyone to feel loved and welcome, and I never want anyone to feel they are less than or left out. I have had people tell me you should not feel that way "You are the daughter of the King!" "You should walk in there with confidence." As I have grown in age and wisdom, I am better about such environments, but it is not my comfortable place.

I despise haughtiness and pride as it makes others feel less which is a tactic of the enemy to create comparison and insecurity. That is how I know comparison is a tactic of the enemy. If you compare any two people with anything, someone will always be made to feel less than the other.

Once when Tom and I were waiting on a flight at LAX, there was a fancy steakhouse in the newer part of the airport that Tom wanted to take me to. I took one look and immediately felt uncomfortable. It just did not feel warm and welcoming to me, only to the elite. I opted for a pizza instead, hanging out in a relaxed part of the airport.

I do not want anyone to walk out of my church because they do not feel welcome or loved, or because they feel uncomfortable. That would be a tragedy. I want people to feel welcome so they can encounter the love, saving, and healing power of Jesus Christ.

As you walk into the foyer of our church, one of the first things you see is a large hanging sign on the wall saying, "Welcome Home." And that sign is what you see after you have already been greeted by several warm, smiling faces and friendly voices. I feel so blessed every time people say to me, "I felt so loved the moment I first walked into your church. I felt at home."

In writing this, I am thinking to myself, "Now that is Godly hospitality."

Godly hospitality is modeled for us in the Bible so we can see the importance of both the heart and feet of hospitality. We read about it in one of the most well-known Bible stories used to teach about hospitality, the story of Martha and Mary.

The story of Martha and Mary is found in Luke 10:38-42. *"Now it happened as they went that He entered a certain village, and a certain woman named Martha welcomed Him into her house. And she had a sister called Mary, who also sat at Jesus' feet and heard His word. But Martha was distracted with much serving, and she approached Him and said, "Lord, do you not care that my sister has left me to serve alone? Therefore, tell her to help me." And Jesus answered and said to her. "Martha, Martha, you are worried and troubled about many things. But one thing is needed, and Mary is chosen that good part, which will not be taken away from her."*

What I find interesting about this story is that Martha seems to be the one that is being hospitable, while Mary might be perceived to be lazy and inconsiderate. But when you think of the definition of hospitality, "the friendly and generous reception and entertainment of guests, visitors and strangers," and when we acknowledge the Biblical word that says, *"In humility, we are to value others above ourselves,"* found in Philippians 2:4, we can begin to view this story with a unique perspective.

The first thing the Lord showed me is the position and location where Mary was sitting. She was sitting at His feet. There is no greater position of humility than at one's feet. It shows us that she was valuing and honoring Jesus. It also says she *"heard His word."* The word "heard" used here in the Greek means to "attend to" or "to consider" or maybe we can even say, "be considerate." This sounds like hospitality to me. She gave Him an audience.

In other words, "Jesus, you are the most important thing in the room. You are our guest. And you have my full attention." And *she listened to the word*, in the Greek means, "uttered by a living voice." Can you imagine? The true and the living God in the flesh, speaking a word. How could one not sit at His feet and listen? How could you be drawn away by things not near as important as cleaning and washing dishes? It can be difficult for many women as we seek our identity on perfection instead of position.

As we continue in the text it speaks of *Martha being distracted by much serving*. The word distracted in Greek means "to be cumbered or held back, weighted down, too busy, or drawn away" (by the ministry). How many of you know we can be drawn away by ministry or busyness?

I remember a time in my early Christian life being so busy with the ministry I had no time to sit at the feet of Jesus. I admit, I was too busy and distracted to humble myself and take the time to give Him an audience. If we do not learn this valuable lesson of hospitality, how can we even hear His voice or the voice of our guest's conversations?

I remember a Pastor telling me it was comparable to me running around the church doing ministry. Jesus walks up and taps me on the shoulder, and I ignore Him saying, "Don't bother me, I'm busy serving God." I am sure His response to me would be a lot like Jesus speaking to Martha and asking the question *Who are you really serving*?

How can I be serving God when I have no time to attend to Him and enjoy His very presence and the reason we gather? If we are too busy with ministry tasks, how can we properly attend to God or His people?

We also cannot allow our rules to become more important than people. In the Kingdom of God, this is a grave error occurring. There have been many times I have personally witnessed people being made to feel less valuable than rules, protocols, or tasks that need to be fulfilled. We cannot allow ourselves to be distracted from what is most important, God and people! The greatest commandment is *"To love the Lord your God with all your heart soul and strength and to love your neighbor as yourself"* found in Mark 12:30 and Luke 10:27. The lesson has been taught to us often in the Bible and so I am sure it is important!

I will never forget attending a small church where we had regular weekly outreach events. Outreach is for the sole purpose of inviting and ministering to people to lead them to Christ so they can be saved and healed.

During the day we would walk the streets and invite people to our Saturday night live event with our worship band singing and the Gospel would be preached with an invitation for people to receive Christ at the end of service.

One Saturday night we had only one visitor. Yes, I said one. A young mother with three children. As the service went on the children were a little rambunctious and out of control. I was shocked when two of the ushers went up to her and said, "We are going to have to ask you to take your children outside as they are a distraction." What? The one person in the room who did not yet know Christ was asked to leave because her children were out of control. Talk about missing service and showing hospitality! Some of the saints should have instead shown hospitality and helped with the children allowing her to hear and receive the word of God. We should have honored her and served her at that moment. But instead, rules were made more important than the person.

Ministry is never more important than loving, honoring, and valuing people. We are to host them by showing them by our actions they are the most valuable thing in the room. Our hospitality is inspired through our love for them, and they will know it because we live it.

If I were to summarize in just a few words what Godly hospitality means to me, it would be this; let everything you do, be done in love. Learn to love people the way Jesus loves them and then serve them the way He did when He walked the Earth.

I believe if we love and honor people the way God would have us to, the most excellent hospitality would be the result. Greet people with welcoming warmth and smiles. Serve their favorite delicious food with the most skillfully prepared hands and hearts. Set the atmosphere and decorate in a way that makes them feel welcome, valued, and loved. Play their favorite music and light their favorite candle.

What can you think of? And how can you use your gifts to bless them? Our hospitality will only go as deep as our love for ourselves and God's people. 1 Peter 4:8-9 *"Above all, love each other deeply because love covers a multitude of sins. And offer hospitality to one another without grumbling."* Hospitality should never be a chore, but a natural result of our love for one another. In Luke 10, Martha was troubled and worried about many things, while Mary showed love and gave honor to her Lord. Do not sweat the perfection of your décor my friend, look the people around you in their eyes and love them with all your strength, in every little thing you do and say, and you will develop and live out the Godly characteristic of hospitality.

Group Discussion Questions

1. What was your idea of hospitality before reading this chapter? Share with the group and discuss.

2. How would you define Godly hospitality? Be specific and discuss.

3. Do you consider yourself to have the gift of hospitality? Why or why not?

4. Share a time you felt you were shown excellent hospitality and why? Discuss with the group.

5. Can you name any other characters in the Bible that showed hospitality as defined in this chapter?

6. Have your thoughts about showing hospitality changed since reading this chapter? How? Share and discuss.

Homework

1. Study Philippians 2:3-4. What is God revealing to you in this scripture about the way we should show hospitality? Are there any changes you will make in the future because of what you understand this scripture to mean?

   _____
   _____
   _____
   _____

2. 1 Peter 4:9 says "*Offer hospitality to one another without grumbling.*" In Greek grumbling means "secret displeasure." Do you feel in some circumstances it would be difficult to offer hospitality without secret displeasure? Pray and ask God to show you how to overcome this. Write down the reasons you think you will be able to show hospitality to all people.

   _____
   _____
   _____
   _____

3. Read Colossians 3:23-24 "*Whatever you do, work at it with all your heart, as working for the Lord, not for human masters, since you know that you will receive an inheritance from the Lord as a reward. It is the Lord Christ you are serving.*" Pray and ask Him for a transformed heart of hospitality. Write what He shares with you.

   _____
   _____
   _____
   _____

4. Pray and ask God to speak to you about what you can learn from Mary in Luke chapter 10. Write down everything the Lord shows you and meditate on it. Read it often and ask God to change your heart to serve like Jesus.

5. Plan a get-together with someone you are just getting to know, someone you feel God has brought into your life. Or if you like, plan a get-together with a friend. Plan ways to show them Godly hospitality. After this experience write down the ways this made both of you feel. What was the fruit of your hospitality?

6. Read John 13:35. Write a paragraph on how this scripture applies to hospitality?

7. What does humility have to do with hospitality? Read John 13:2-5,14 and write a paragraph on what Jesus was trying to teach the disciples by performing this act.

Daily Prayer to Develop this Characteristic:

Dear Father, create in me a heart of hospitality and renew a spirit of love and right service within me. Father, I desire to focus on you and your amazing love for us in all that I do to serve others whether in home, business, or community. Lord, reflect in me the things you want me to do like Mary and to learn to lay down the things that are distracting me or keeping my eyes from you and focusing on you like Mary. Take away the business and distractions of life when I am trying to serve you. Father, make me a new woman with a great gift of hospitality and make all feel your warmth and love.

Lord, I thank you for creating me so perfectly and considering every detail in who you created me to be. Thank you for showing me how valuable my life is by sending your only Son to die on the cross for me. I know I was created to make a difference in this world.

Thank you for the example you gave us through the life of Jesus. Fill my heart with the love of God and help me to love and serve others as Jesus did. As I go through my days show me how I can show love and honor people by even the smallest actions I take. Help me to show hospitality to all people and to not ever be a judge or respecter of persons. I thank you Father for teaching me to love and host others like you! Thank you for developing the gift of hospitality in me. In Christ's name Amen.

Journal Your Own Prayer:

_____
_____
_____
_____
_____
_____
_____
_____
_____
_____
_____
_____
_____
_____
_____
_____
_____
_____
_____

Godly Characteristic #12
Stewardship

Any enterprise is built by wise planning, becomes strong through common sense, and profits wonderfully by keeping abreast of the facts.

Proverbs 24:3-4

Cathy Guerrero

Regency Christian Church International, Whittier, CA
Founder of Life Builder Seminars

Cathy and her husband, Dr. Jason Guerrero, founded Regency Christian Center International in 1979, a local church, training center, and center of spiritual life for families and individuals. Together, they pastored, counseled, educated, and built people until Jason transitioned to Heaven in February 2019. As a leader who understands legacy, Cathy transitioned the leadership of the church to the next generation of Senior Leaders, Jim and Renee Cutter, in August 2019. She continues to function as the Overseer of Regency Christian Center International.

Cathy is the founder of Life Builders Seminars, a women's ministry dedicated to building the lives of women with the Word of God, currently eight chapters meeting in LA, Orange, and San Diego counties, as well as Mexico.

Cathy has a bachelor's degree in theology, a Master of Arts in Theology degree in Professional Christian Counseling, and a Doctorate Degree from Vision Christian University. She was a teaching faculty member for Regency Bible College, teaching faculty for the Institute of Christian Counseling, and an adjunct professor at Vision Christian University.

Cathy ministers nationally as well as internationally in the Philippines, New Zealand, Fiji, Japan, South America, and West Africa.

Stewardship

Learning to steward our lives and walk-in wisdom begins by aligning our decision-making with the word of God. Let us begin in Proverbs 24:3-4 NLT *"Any enterprise is built by wise planning, becomes strong through common sense and profits wonderfully by keeping abreast of the facts"*. This scripture teaches us that planning builds, wisdom strengthens, and facts profit.

Built by Wise Planning

An enterprise is defined as an undertaking, especially one of some scope, complication, and risk; the willingness to undertake new ventures with initiative; industrious, systematic activity, especially when directed toward profit, or a business organization.

An enterprise does not just happen on its own. An enterprise is developed with a purpose in mind. When we set a goal or want to realize a dream, we need a plan. Plans are the direction for success. Whether we are building the enterprise of relationship, marriage, business, education, or ministry, we need a vision and a plan. Plans strategically anchor your vision to the purpose.

We find tremendous principles for vision and planning in Habakkuk 2:1-3 *'I will stand my watch and set myself on the rampart and watch to see what He will say to me, and what I will answer when I am corrected. Then the LORD answered me and said: "Write the vision and make it plain on tablets, that He may run who reads it. For the vision is yet for an appointed time, But at the end, it will speak, and it will not lie. Though it tarries, wait for it; Because it will surely come, it will not tarry."*

Let us examine six principles that we can use in everyday life to clarify our personal vision and plan.

1. Set yourself apart and position yourself to hear from God.

We will have many ideas, thoughts, and passions, however, what does God have in His heart that will cause remarkable success? I have found over the years that my greatest imagining pales in comparison to the Lord's purpose. He will take us to a place of fulfillment, but first He wants to enlarge our capacity for success and train us to implement for the Kingdom. God is the supernatural architect, and we are His instrument.

Find your place to meet with God and make that your altar area. It may be your sofa or if you are a busy mom, it may be in your car parked in the driveway.

I have friends that would meet daily at the kitchen sink to pray as a couple. That was their altar of meeting. After a few years of praying in the kitchen, the presence of God was so tangible that everyone who entered that kitchen would sense Him there. God will reside where we make Him welcome.

2. Be open to God's voice.

It is remarkably interesting how Habakkuk uses the term "I will watch to see what He will say to me." So many times, we hear from God in pictures. I love the old saying: *a picture is worth a thousand words*. When a picture comes to mind, we can mistakenly dismiss it as our imagination rather than a deposit of revelation. When we have a mind that has been sanctified, we will know what God is, what is our thoughts and what is our enemy. That is why we must acknowledge that we who belong to Him have the mind of Christ.

1 Corinthians 2:16 *"For who has known the mind of the LORD that He may instruct Him? But we have the mind of Christ."*

There is so much truth that we can miss when we believe that God's voice is something that only certain people hear. God clearly states in John 10:27 that His sheep hear His voice.

I remember when I heard God directing me to start a new women's ministry. The vision that the Lord gave me was unlike any women's ministry model that I had known. As a Pastor, my paradigm consisted of women's ministry *in the church*. I had been doing that for many years, and I was sensing that He wanted to take it in another direction.

This ministry was to build women who would not come to another church for fear that they would dishonor their home church by attending another denomination. This ministry was to build women who may not necessarily enter a church building. He introduced me to this foreign paradigm. I laugh now because my initial thoughts were, "Lord, are you sure you are talking to the right person?" Instantly the what-ifs and the how can this be entered. This brings us to the next principle.

3. Be willing to adjust.

As the download of possibility came, I found myself understanding that if I was going to be obedient and fulfill His purpose, then I needed to adjust myself to His plan. The principle of new wineskins is about being able to stretch to hold the new. New flexible skins have been rubbed with oil just as the Holy Spirit rubs us with the oil of His presence to prepare us for growth.

Mark 2:22 *"And no one puts new wine into old wineskins; or else the new wine bursts the wineskins, the wine is spilled, and the wineskins are ruined. But new wine must be put into new wineskins."*

When we are willing to be used in new dimensions it will take a bit of faith risk. I remember when the Lord had a prophetic word for a young businessperson in our church. The portion of the word that so impacted me was, "Faith is risky business, but it is never a gamble." How many times I have reflected on this, reminding myself that faith does take the risk to step out of the boat, but it is never a gamble. If we want to walk on water, we must be willing to get out of the boat and trust Him. God will make even the water solid beneath our feet if He calls us out of the boat. God will never gamble with our lives; His word is as sure as the foundation of His Kingdom.

4. Then the Lord answered.

When we position ourselves to hear and listen to what He has to say, He will give the directive. It may come all at once or over a period. Sometimes it is like the process of developing film, the picture becomes clearer with time. God is faithful to give us what is necessary for the time and season. We can be sure that God will answer us.

Jeremiah 33:3 *"Call to Me, and I will answer you, and show you great and mighty things, which you do not know."*

We can also expect to receive more answers and direction from the Lord as we remain faithful. When we are faithful in one area He will begin to add increasingly.

Matthew 25:23 *"His lord said to Him, 'Well done, good and faithful servant; you have been faithful over a few things, I will make you ruler over many things. Enter into the joy of your lord.'"*

5. Write the plan.

Planning is imperative to success. A plan is an articulated action outlining the steps needed to arrive at a set goal or vision. Every well-organized institution and enterprise has a plan. Businesses, schools, churches, governments, and even nations formulate strategically written plans to succeed.

By failing to prepare, you are preparing to fail. -Benjamin Franklin

When we put pen to paper to clarify the vision solidifies within. This is our tangible faith in action. As we read, rehearse, and run with the vision we must position ourselves in faith as God brings all the persons and parts together.

At times, the vision may seem stagnant or unattainable. Continue in faith obedience knowing that His perfect plan includes others that may be in preparation just as you have been in preparation. We may not see the whole picture, yet it will unfold as the vision develops.

6. Do not give up. God has perfect timing.

We must remember that God usually makes us ready for what He is bringing to us. The more responsibility that comes with the vision and the plan, the more maturing it takes on our part.

I had always considered myself mature, and in some areas I was. In many other areas, I was not. How do we treat others? How do we navigate through the storms of life? What are our motives? What are our priorities? How balanced is our life? Is our family in order? Are we a person who will not bend, bow, or compromise our core values and principles?

Planning aids our maturity process. We must first plan to be committed to God and His purposes. When our outer goals are established and become our inner commitment, we have begun to mature. Systems are important, and character counts!

Wisdom Strengthens

Wikipedia defines "wisdom" as the ability to think and act using knowledge, experience, understanding, common sense, and insight.

Wisdom often requires managing our emotions, allowing reason to prevail and determine our actions. Wisdom is a disposition to find the truth, coupled with optimum judgment to determine the actions that should be taken to deliver the correct outcome.

Common sense is not so common. -Voltaire

Proverbs 4:7 *"The beginning of wisdom is: get (skillful and godly) wisdom! (For skillful and godly wisdom is the principal thing.) And with all you have gotten, get understanding (discernment, comprehension, and interpretation)."*

Common sense is genius dressed up in work clothes. -Ralph Waldo Emerson

Core values are the constant, Biblical, core beliefs that drive your life, your mission, your vision, and your plan. When we compromise and deviate from our core values, we walk away from wisdom, and it is an indicator that we have lost focus on what is important. At which point we are unable to properly move forward.

Our core values influence our involvement, interest, and integrity. Our core values will always stay in alignment with wisdom. Knowing our core values and adhering to them allows us to change or adjust to anything new or different while standing strong and unmovable. One of my favorite quotes is from Oral Roberts, "I am never willing to change my principle, but I am always willing to change my method."

When wisdom operates at the core of your plan you will continue forwarding momentum. When others are at a stalemate, you will be able to take purposeful steps toward accomplishment.

Proverbs 8:15 *"by (wisdom) kings reign, and rulers decree justice."*

Wisdom, wise planning, and good sense are the guide and rules to succeeding in your pursuit of divine purpose. We must continue to submit our thought processes and emotions to the word of God. Even as Jesus grew in every area, we must also continue to grow in wisdom and understanding. Doing so brings God's favor to us and our enterprise.

Luke 2:52 "A*nd Jesus increased in wisdom (in broad and full understanding) and in stature and years, and favor with God and man.*"

Wisdom is a tool that God uses for promotion and honor. In Genesis 41, we see the process that Joseph went through to grow from a young dreamer to a mature developer. Joseph was promoted from a prison inmate to second in command to fulfill His divine destiny, to save the family and a nation. Joseph surmounted many difficulties and challenges, yet never vacillated from His core values. He was proven and developed along the journey.

> **Our core values influence our involvement, interest, and integrity. Our core values will always stay in alignment with wisdom.**

In Daniel 3, wisdom was working in Daniel, Meshach, Shadrach, and Abednego to promote them to leadership positions in the land of Babylon and Persia. Wisdom will cause us to be successful in our life and enterprise.

Proverbs 4:7-9 *"Wisdom is supreme; therefore, get wisdom. Though it cost all you have, get understanding. Esteem her, and she will exalt you; embrace her, and she will honor you. She will set a garland of grace on your head and present you with a crown of splendor."*

Facts Profit

We must honestly appraise our position or situation while focusing on the vision.

Facts are benchmarks we can utilize to track our performance and make midcourse adjustments, as necessary. As we continually assess the facts, we keep the vision before us, and we bring that vision into the present by and through faith. Lance Wallnau states, "Real leaders do not avoid reality, they confront the brutal facts. They see reality but do not surrender to it."

Ignorance is not bliss; ignorance can be dangerous. Keeping records and knowing the condition of what you are building, or overseeing is necessary to becoming profitable. If we do not have the information or knowledge, we must be willing to do the research and learn. Also, remember that partial facts are not conclusive. Facts often contain layers of the pertinent information needed to evaluate properly.

Hence, it is imperative to stay connected to those who keep you abreast of the facts you may not otherwise discover. Facts do not cease to exist just because they are unknown or ignored. If we put our head in the sand like an ostrich, we become an exposed target, positioned for failure to give us a big kick in the behind.

Can you imagine boarding an airplane and hearing that the crew forgot to check the condition of the engine, wheels, or landing gear? How about forgetting to check the fuel? Just as you would want to ensure your safety in the air, we want to make sure that our enterprise is in order. Truthful evaluation is critical to any building process. Without the facts, we are flying blind. Without the facts, we can lose our direction, hit the wall, and self-destruct.

Luke 14:28 *"But do not begin until you count the cost. For which one of you would begin construction of a building without first getting estimates and then checking to see if there is enough money to pay the bills?"*

My Story

The year 2000 was a season of walking through uncharted waters. My incredible husband had been challenged with exceedingly difficult long-term health issues and needed to receive a liver transplant. He and I had been Senior Leads of our local church for two decades. We had quite a bit on our plates, and this was the time that the Lord began to speak to me about making an entire paradigm shift in my approach to women's ministry.

God began to seed me with thoughts and ideas that just did not fit into my ministry experience. He stretched me in a way that made me want to dance and scream at the same time. As I spent time in His presence and wrote down what He showed me, He began to prepare me.

I shared it with several mature women and asked them to pray with me for His timing and strategy. Thank God for women who will partner to press into the vision, and not pull away because of opposing opinions.

God was guiding me to approach the ministry in such a way that it would reach beyond the church building. A new ministry model, a safe place for women to gather and be equipped and empowered for life. His heart was to prepare women to lead. First themselves, then their homes and workplaces. Empower women to lead in their local church with wisdom and strength, without being competitive or combative.

This was the beginning of building the enterprise. Understanding that what God wanted to accomplish entailed a seminar framework for imparting truth and wisdom principles. The focus of the seminars would not be confined to a gathering for fellowship only. Now how would that look and where were we going to get the finances to take this seminar to a public venue?

We implemented Habakkuk 2:1-3 and the process began. Now I must say that it did not come overnight, it was developed over time.

I began to look for the venue, many sites in many cities. Each time walking in the door was a genuine experience in and of itself. I began to sense so many things, evaluating the space, cleanliness, leasing availability, parking, and the spiritual atmosphere. Wanting to have monthly recurring seminars narrowed the field quickly.

It would have been more convenient to have it in our church, not to mention that there would not have been a financial commitment involved. Yet, God had made it noticeably clear to me that a church venue was not His heart for what we would need to achieve.

After much exploration, we ended up with a contract for the Brea Civic Center. This is the venue we have had since the inception of Life Builder Seminars. I would like to shout out and thank Nicole Andrews, the Community Services Supervisor we have worked with all these years.

Now that we had found a venue, we needed to think about the topics and how we would present information applicable to daily life and share keys to developing and growing in a relationship with the Lord. The vision was for a word-based, practical, and non-superficial seminar.

I also knew that we needed to give a platform to women who had a gift to teach yet had never received opportunities to hone their gifts. God was tremendously gracious to show me that there needed to be two speaking sessions each seminar, one topic with two different teachers and their individual perspectives. This allowed us to teach speakers how to prepare notes to accompany their teaching. These notes were prepared as handouts for attendees to keep, review, and apply.

This seminar model has been one of the most incredible tools that we have ever seen to strengthen speaking and writing skills. The vision was a unique niche.

We also structured teams to teach women how to lead and develop others. We have a team leader for each area of the seminar. Each leader then trains a team to serve and oversees them, to develop new leaders.

As we were faithful to steward well and develop what God provided, He began to add to us each meeting. After a few years, women began to contact me and ask how they could start a seminar in their city. The multiplication began.

Proverbs 24:3-4 *"Wise people are builders – They build families, business, and communities. And through intelligence and insight, their enterprises are established and endure. Because of their skilled leadership, the hearts of people are filled with the treasures of wisdom and the pleasures of spiritual wealth."*

Good Stewardship

Good stewardship, defined as the careful and responsible management of something entrusted to one's care, is imperative to growth. A good steward cultivates integrity, commitment, and efficiency. I call it the ICE principle. Intentional integrity is the result of trained character responding in moral excellence in every situation.

Integrity

Oxford Dictionary's definition of "integrity" is the quality of being honest and having strong moral principles, moral uprightness. The state of being whole and undivided, the condition of being unified, unimpaired.

Integrity is doing the right thing, even when no one is watching. -C.S. Lewis

Integrity is living a life consistent with the principles of God's character. It prevents us from falling into the trap of compartmentalizing life, so we are one thing in some settings and something else in others. Integrity is a product of fearing God and exemplifies what a relationship with God looks like to those who are watching us.

Integrity commits itself to character over personal gain or interests. People are a priority over things, service becomes powerful, principle always trumps convenience, and the long term outweighs the immediate.

A good steward has a lifestyle of intentional integrity. Knowing that God has given us oversight to build His Kingdom, which impacts generations to come.

Commitment

Commitment is being dedicated to a cause. We are to count the cost and be willing to follow through. Are we willing to do what it takes to see the vision fulfilled?

Long-term goals require commitment and focus because when the enthusiasm for a new thing wears off and it is no longer fun, self-discipline kicks in. We must always keep in mind our purpose, mandate, and mission to keep the passion alive.

Ecclesiastes 7:8 *"Endings are better than beginnings. Sticking to it is better than standing out."*

Optical Fusion is an interesting term meaning the combining of images from the two eyes to form a single visual percept. Scripture speaks of not being double-minded.

James 1:8 *"He is a double-minded man, unstable in all His ways."*

Double-minded here is *dipsychos* in Greek, meaning two souls. If we cannot focus, we will be unstable and unable to attain the vision.

Another type of Optical Fusion is combining God's sight with my sight, to have His perspective. It is God's vision and our vision becoming one.

Without commitment, we will not have focus. Without focus, there will be no commitment.

Hebrews 6:11 *"And now I want each of you to extend that same intensity toward a full-bodied hope and keep it to the end."*

Efficiency

Efficient is being capable of producing desired results with little. or no waste, being well organized, competent, and resourceful, making the most of every situation, doing our best, and always seeking better ways to be a good steward in all that we do.

Good stewards are productive to honor God, are well organized, and manage resources, gifts, and talent well. Whatever we do, let us do it with all our heart to magnify God.

Martin Luther King Jr. said, *"If a man is called to be a street sweeper, He should sweep streets even as Michelangelo painted, or Beethoven composed music or Shakespeare wrote poetry. He should sweep streets so well that all the hosts of Heaven and Earth will pause to say, here lived a great street sweeper who did his job well."*

We can either spend or invest our time. Once it is spent, we do not get it back. When we invest with the intention it is a seed that produces. A conscious steward is interested in personal growth. We cannot give what we do not possess. Lifelong learner tends to stay fresh as they challenge themselves to grow and increase. I do not know about you, but I want to live until I die.

Psalms 90:12 *"So teach us to number our days, that we may gain a heart of wisdom."*

Sharpen your ax when it is dull. We have all heard to *work smarter, not harder*. Still, some struggle in vain not perceiving the areas that need to be examined and sharpened.

Ecclesiastes 10:10 *"If the ax is dull, and one does not sharpen the edge, then He must use more strength; But wisdom brings success."*

This is when we find that sustaining good relationships and oversight is beneficial. When we allow others to speak into our lives and help us to see our blind spots, it will keep us from spinning our wheels for little or no results.

This reminds me of the portion of scripture in 2 Kings 6:1-7 where we see the notable example of Elisha mentoring the young students under his direction. I have used the principles in this portion of scripture to build and establish in my own life, and to mentor others.

2 Kings 6:1-7 *"And the sons of the prophets said to Elisha, "See now, the place where we dwell with you is too small for us. Please, let us go to the Jordan, and let every man take a beam from there, and let us make there a place where we may dwell." So, he answered, "Go." Then one said, "Please consent to go with your servants." And he answered, "I will go." So, he went with them. And when they came to the Jordan, they cut down trees. But as one was cutting down a tree, the iron ax head fell into the water; and he cried out and said, "Alas, master! For it was borrowed." So, the man of God said, "Where did it fall?" And he showed him the place. So, he cut off a stick, and threw it in there; and he made the iron float. Therefore, he said, "Pick it up for yourself." So, he reached out his hand and took it."*

Let us look at a few of these principles:

1. Recognize when we need to expand, having outgrown the place where you are. *"And the sons of the prophets said to Elisha, "See now, the place where we dwell with you is too small for us."*

2. Be willing to work to develop the larger vision, and do not come out from under your covering. The experience of your oversight is a great benefit to your success. *"Please, let us go to the Jordan, and let every man take a beam from there, and let us make there a place where we may dwell."*

3. When your vision is from God others will recognize it and be willing to support your endeavor to accomplish something greater for the Kingdom. *"So, he answered, "Go." Then one said, "Please consent to go with your servants."*

4. When we give our word, make sure to fulfill it. Do not vacillate midstream. *"And he answered, "I will go." So, he went with them."*

5. Stay within the grace that God has given you. Do not try to wear another's armor by borrowing their tools. Use what is given to you. *"But as one was cutting down a tree, the iron ax head fell into the water; and he cried out and said, "Alas, master! For it was borrowed."*

6. Stay transparent and accountable to those who are your covering.

7. A true leader will ask the right questions to help you find the solution. *"So, the man of God said, "Where did it fall?"*

8. Be willing to humble yourself, stay transparent, and adjust. *"And he showed him the place."*

9. When we look to the cross, symbolized by the stick in this scripture, we will see miracles in our lives. *"So, he cut off a stick, and threw it in there; and he made the iron float."*

10. A good leader or mentor will always help you to see what needs to be done and empower you to apply truth. Empowerment is not enablement; we must know what and how to do it for ourselves to grow and develop. *"Therefore, he said, "Pick it up for yourself." So, he reached out his hand and took it."*

Each one of us is called to build and establish the Kingdom of God through our arena of influence. With the grace of God and His oversight, we can accomplish more than we can imagine.

Ephesians 3:20 *"Now to him who can do exceedingly abundantly above all that we ask or think, according to the power that works in us."*

Let us take the challenge to grow personally and develop our gifts and talents to influence and impact our sphere of authority. You are called, anointed, and commissioned to be His hand extended, and His voice of revelation.

I am convinced we have much to look ahead to. Let us, partner, together and see it accomplished.

Group Discussion Questions

1. Have you established a place to meet with God regularly? Explain and share with the group.

2. How do you hear from God? Be specific and write it down.

3. Have you written down your God-given vision and mission to plan? What is it and have you shared it with anyone? Why or why not?

4. What are your core values? Write them down and pray on them daily. Share with the group.

5. Who have you connected with to develop depth of wisdom? Share.

6. How do you exhibit efficiency in your daily life? Discuss with your group.

7. Who do you trust to be an accountability partner? Why?

8. Do you allow your accountability partner to speak into your life? How? Discuss with the group.

Homework

1. Write down Proverbs 24:3-4 and commit it to memory by repeating it daily this week.

2. When you spend time with the Lord, listen for His voice and write down what He says to you. As you journal you will begin to see His direction for you. Jeremiah 33:3 *"Call to Me, and I will answer you, and show you great and mighty things, which you do not know."*

3. Write down what God shows you and discern what He is speaking to you through the picture. Habakkuk 2:1 *"I will stand my watch and set myself on the rampart and watch to see what He will say to me, and what I will answer when I am corrected."*

4. Write down the areas that you recognize need adjustment. What will you do to accomplish these adjustments?

5. How will you apply the ICE principle- integrity, commitment, and efficiency?

6. Write down the areas in your life that are being developed through integrity. Be specific and write it in detail.

7. Ask God to show you where you need to evaluate your commitment level to the assignment that He has entrusted to you.

8. What can you do to sharpen your ax for better efficiency? Ecclesiastes 10:10 *"If the ax is dull, and one does not sharpen the edge, then He must use more strength; But wisdom brings success."*

Daily Prayer to Develop this Characteristic:

Lord Jesus, I thank you that I have been given gifts to steward, and you have entrusted me to establish your Kingdom. Thank you for the wisdom and grace to fulfill the vision that you have given. I say that I have ears to hear and eyes to see according to your word, your will, and your way. As you lead me, I will follow and be willing to adjust as you give instruction.

According to Isaiah 50:4-5 "You have given me the tongue of the learned that I should know to speak a word in season to Him that is weary. You awaken me morning by morning to hear as the learned, and I say that I will not be rebellious or turn away. What you have assigned me to do, I will do."

I have hidden your word in my heart, that I may know how to walk in wisdom and give honor to you in all that I do. You order my steps and connect me with the right people in the right season for the right purpose. I yield myself to Holy Spirit to be a person of integrity, commitment, and effectiveness. I pray Lord, that I am a good steward with my life in every arena. Please lead me, guide me, and direct my steps along the path. In Jesus' name, Amen.

Journal Your Own Prayer:

CELEBRATION AND TESTIMONY WRITING

LEADER GUIDE

KICK-OFF

DISCUSSION STARTER. After meeting others in the group, encourage women to discuss what drew them to the study and the title *12 Characteristics of a Godly Woman*. Discuss what they expect to get out of the study. Discuss what is their level of commitment? The more they commit to each week's reading and homework, the more they will grow and develop in these Godly characteristics

WATCH the WELCOME VIDEO FROM TAMARA on www.GodsAmazingPlans.com

EMPHASIZE THE IMPORTANCE OF COMMITTING TO SPENDING TIME DAILY AND CREATING THE HABIT OF SEEKING THE LORD. Have each one share ideas to encourage others of when and where to commit time with Jesus daily throughout this study. Point out the value of creating this time for their personal growth and transformation.

GROUP DISCUSSIONS. Have someone read aloud each question or pick several to discuss with one another as time permits. Create participation and conversation by sharing ideas and encourage each together as they commit to their twelve-week transformational study.

HOMEWORK: Encourage them to make the weekly commitment so they can spend time daily in the presence of their Father. Start today with daily prayer, worship, and journaling. Encourage them to read it daily and pray over what they have written and ask God to start preparing their hearts and mind to hear from Him.

Assign reading chapter 1 in preparation for next week's study. If you think it would work better for your group, you can also read the chapter in the study and then only assign the Homework for them during the week.

Be creative and customize what works best for your group of women.

Chapter 1: SEEK GOD FIRST

DISCUSSION STARTER. After prayer and worship, review what they learned as they read chapter 1 authored by Tamara Doss last week. If you are choosing to read the chapter in the study, ask women to read several paragraphs and go around the room until you have finished the chapter. Encourage women to discuss what they experienced during the week of study and journaling.

BIBLE STUDY #1 MEMORY VERSE:
Matthew 6:33-34 *"But seek first the Kingdom and His righteousness, and all these things will be given to you as well. Therefore, do not worry about tomorrow, for tomorrow will worry about itself. Each day has enough trouble of its own."*

WATCH SESSION 1 VIDEO at www.GodsAmazingPlans.com

GROUP DISCUSSIONS. Refer to page 31 and review group discussion questions. You can break into smaller groups for discussion to encourage deeper sharing. Have each of them answer the questions and share for encouragement.

HOMEWORK Encourage them to take time for the Homework on page 32 and make the weekly commitment so they can spend time daily in the presence of their Father. Start today with daily prayer, worship, and journaling. Encourage them to read it daily and pray over what they have written and ask God to start preparing their hearts and mind to hear from Him.

Assign reading chapter 2 in preparation for next week's study. If you think it would work better for your group, you can also read the chapter in the study.

Be creative and customize what works best for your group of women.

Chapter 2: LOVE UNCONDITIONALLY

DISCUSSION STARTER. After prayer and worship, review what they learned as they studied last week's session. Encourage women to discuss what they experienced during the week of study and journaling.

BIBLE STUDY MEMORY VERSE:
Matthew 22:35-40 *"One of them, an expert in the law, tested Him with this question; "Teacher, which is the greatest commandment in the Law?"*

WATCH SESSION 2 VIDEO at www.GodsAmazingPlans.com

GROUP DISCUSSIONS. Refer to page 46 and review group discussion questions. You can break into smaller groups for discussion to encourage deeper sharing. Have each of them answer the questions and share for encouragement.

HOMEWORK. Encourage them to take time for the Homework on page 48 and to make the weekly commitment so they can spend time daily in the presence of their Father. Start today with daily prayer, worship, and journaling. Encourage them to read it daily and pray over what they have written and ask God to start preparing their hearts and mind to hear from Him.

Assign reading chapter 3 in preparation for next week's study. If you think it would work better for your group, you can also read the chapter in the study.

Be creative and customize what works best for your group of women.

Chapter 3: PRAYERFUL LIFE

DISCUSSION STARTER. After prayer and worship, review what they learned as they studied last week at the session. Encourage women to discuss what they experienced during the week of study and journaling.

BIBLE STUDY #3 MEMORY VERSE:
Jeremiah 33:3 *"Call to me and I will answer you and tell you great and mighty things you do not know."*

WATCH SESSION 3 VIDEO at www.GodsAmazingPlans.com

GROUP DISCUSSIONS. Refer to page 61 and review group discussion questions. You can break into smaller groups for discussion to encourage deeper sharing. Have each of them answer the questions and share for encouragement.

HOMEWORK. Encourage them to take time for the Homework on page 63 and to make the weekly commitment so they can spend time daily in the presence of their Father. Start today with daily prayer, worship, and journaling. Encourage them to read it daily and pray over what they have written and ask God to start preparing their hearts and mind to hear from Him.

Assign reading chapter 4 in preparation for next week's study. If you think it would work better for your group, you can also read the chapter in the study.

Be creative and customize what works best for your group of women.

Chapter 4: OBEDIENCE

DISCUSSION STARTER. After prayer and Worship, review what they learned as they studied last week's session three and practice committing to their 30 minutes every day. Encourage women to discuss what they experienced during the week of study and journaling.

BIBLE STUDY #4 MEMORY VERSE:
John 14:21 *"Those who truly love me are those who obey my commands. Whoever passionately loves me will be passionately loved by my Father. And I will passionately love you in return and will manifest my life within you."*

WATCH SESSION 4 VIDEO at www.GodsAmazingPlans.com

GROUP DISCUSSIONS. Refer to page 79 and review group discussion questions. You can break into smaller groups for discussion to encourage deeper sharing. Have each of them answer the questions and share for encouragement.

HOMEWORK. Encourage them to take time for the Homework on page 81 and to make the weekly commitment so they can spend time daily in the presence of their Father. Start today with daily prayer, worship, and journaling. Encourage them to read it daily and pray over what they have written and ask God to start preparing their hearts and mind to hear from Him.

Assign reading chapter 5 in preparation for next week's study. If you think it would work better for your group, you can also read the chapter in the study.

Be creative and customize what works best for your group of women.

Chapter 5: FAMILY FIRST

DISCUSSION STARTER. After prayer and worship, review what they learned as they studied last week's session four and practice committing to their 30 minutes every day. Encourage women to discuss what they experienced during the week of study and journaling.

BIBLE STUDY #5 MEMORY VERSE:
Psalm 103:17-18 *"The loving-kindness of the Lord is from everlasting to everlasting in those who reverently fear Him, and His righteousness to children's children, to those who honor and keep His covenant, and remember to do His commandments imprinting His word on their hearts."*

WATCH SESSION 5 VIDEO at www.GodsAmazingPlans.com

GROUP DISCUSSIONS. Refer to page 101 and review group discussion questions. You can break into smaller groups for discussion to encourage deeper sharing. Have each of them answer the questions and share for encouragement.

HOMEWORK. Encourage them to take time for the Homework on page 102 and to make the weekly commitment so they can spend time daily in the presence of their Father. Start today with daily prayer, worship, and journaling. Encourage them to read it daily and pray over what they have written and ask God to start preparing their hearts and mind to hear from Him.

Assign reading chapter 6 in preparation for next week's study. If you think it would work better for your group, you can also read the chapter in the study.

Be creative and customize what works best for your group of women.

Chapter 6: HUMILITY

DISCUSSION STARTER. After prayer and worship, review what they learned as they studied last week's session four and practice committing to their 30 minutes every day. Encourage women to discuss what they experienced during the week of study and journaling.

BIBLE VERSE #6 MEMORY VERSE:
2 Chronicles 7:14 *"If my people who are called by my name humble themselves and pray and seek my face and turn from their wicked ways, then I will hear from heaven and forgive their sin and heal their land."*

WATCH SESSION 6 VIDEO at www.GodsAmazingPlans.com

GROUP DISCUSSIONS. Refer to page 113 and review group discussion questions. You can break into smaller groups for discussion to encourage deeper sharing. Have each of them answer the questions and share for encouragement.

HOMEWORK. Encourage them to take time for the Homework on page 115 and to make the weekly commitment so they can spend time daily in the presence of their Father. Start today with daily prayer, worship, and journaling. Encourage them to read it daily and pray over what they have written and ask God to start preparing their hearts and mind to hear from Him.

Assign reading chapter 7 in preparation for next week's study. If you think it would work better for your group, you can also read the chapter in the study.

Be creative and customize what works best for your group of women.

Chapter 7: SERVANT HEART

DISCUSSION STARTER. After prayer and worship, review what they learned as they studied last week's session four and practice committing to their 30 minutes every day. Encourage women to discuss what they experienced during the week of study and journaling.

BIBLE STUDY # MEMORY VERSE:
Matthew 20:28 *"Just as the Son of Man did not come to be served, but to serve, and to give His life as a ransom for many."*

WATCH SESSION 7 VIDEO at www.GodsAmazingPlans.com

GROUP DISCUSSIONS. Refer to page 130 and review group discussion questions. You can break into smaller groups for discussion to encourage deeper sharing. Have each of them answer the questions and share for encouragement.

HOMEWORK. Encourage them to take time for the Homework on page 131 and to make the weekly commitment so they can spend time daily in the presence of their Father. Start today with daily prayer, worship, and journaling. Encourage them to read it daily and pray over what they have written and ask God to start preparing their hearts and mind to hear from Him.

Assign reading chapter 8 in preparation for next week's study. If you think it would work better for your group, you can also read the chapter in the study.

Be creative and customize what works best for your group of women.

Chapter 8: HONOR AND RESPECT

DISCUSSION STARTER. After prayer and worship, review what they learned as they studied last week's session four and practice committing to their 30 minutes every day. Encourage women to discuss what they experienced during the week of study and journaling.

BIBLE STUDY #8 MEMORY VERSE:
Romans 13:7 *"Give honor esteem and respect to whom honor is due."*

WATCH SESSION 8 VIDEO at www.GodsAmazingPlans.com

GROUP DISCUSSIONS. Refer to page 142 and review group discussion questions. You can break into smaller groups for discussion to encourage deeper sharing. Have each of them answer the questions and share for encouragement.

HOMEWORK. Encourage them to take time for the Homework on page 143 and to make the weekly commitment so they can spend time daily in the presence of their Father. Start today with daily prayer, worship, and journaling. Encourage them to read it daily and pray over what they have written and ask God to start preparing their hearts and mind to hear from Him.

Assign reading chapter 9 in preparation for next week's study. If you think it would work better for your group, you can also read the chapter in the study.

Be creative and customize what works best for your group of women.

Chapter 9: FAITHFULNESS

DISCUSSION STARTER. After prayer and worship, review what they learned as they studied last week's session four and practice committing to their 30 minutes every day. Encourage women to discuss what they experienced during the week of study and journaling.

BIBLE STUDY #9 MEMORY VERSE:
Psalm 89:1-2 *"I will sing of the mercies of the Lord forever; with my mouth, I will make known thy faithfulness to all generations."*

WATCH SESSION 9 VIDEO at www.GodsAmazingPlans.com

GROUP DISCUSSIONS. Refer to page 159 and review group discussion questions. You can break into smaller groups for discussion to encourage deeper sharing. Have each of them answer the questions and share for encouragement.

HOMEWORK. Encourage them to take time for the Homework on page 160 and to make the weekly commitment so they can spend time daily in the presence of their Father. Start today with daily prayer, worship, and journaling. Encourage them to read it daily and pray over what they have written and ask God to start preparing their hearts and mind to hear from Him.

Assign reading chapter 10 in preparation for next week's study. If you think it would work better for your group, you can also read the chapter in the study.

Be creative and customize what works best for your group of women.

Chapter 10: FRUIT OF THE SPIRIT

DISCUSSION STARTER. After prayer and worship, review what they learned as they studied last week's session four and practice committing to their 30 minutes every day. Encourage women to discuss what they experienced during the week of study and journaling.

BIBLE STUDY #10 MEMORY VERSE:
2 Corinthians 9:15 *"Thanks be to God for His indescribable gift!"*

WATCH SESSION 10 VIDEO at www.GodsAmazingPlans.com

GROUP DISCUSSIONS. Refer to page 176 and review group discussion questions. You can break into smaller groups for discussion to encourage deeper sharing. Have each of them answer the questions and share for encouragement.

HOMEWORK. Encourage them to take time for the Homework on page 177 and to make the weekly commitment so they can spend time daily in the presence of their Father. Start today with daily prayer, worship, and journaling. Encourage them to read it daily and pray over what they have written and ask God to start preparing their hearts and mind to hear from Him.

Assign reading chapter 11 in preparation for next week's study. If you think it would work better for your group, you can also read the chapter in the study.

Be creative and customize what works best for your group of women.

Chapter 11: HOSPITALITY

DISCUSSION STARTER. After prayer and worship, review what they learned as they studied last week's session four and practice committing to their 30 minutes every day. Encourage women to discuss what they experienced during the week of study and journaling.

BIBLE STUDY #11 MEMORY VERSE:
1 Peter 4:8-9 *Above all, love each other deeply because love covers a multitude of sins. Offer hospitality to one another without grumbling.*

WATCH SESSION 11 VIDEO at www.GodsAmazingPlans.com

GROUP DISCUSSIONS. Refer to page 192 and review group discussion questions. You can break into smaller groups for discussion to encourage deeper sharing. Have each of them answer the questions and share for encouragement.

HOMEWORK. Encourage them to take time for the Homework on page 193 and to make the weekly commitment so they can spend time daily in the presence of their Father. Start today with daily prayer, worship, and journaling. Encourage them to read it daily and pray over what they have written and ask God to start preparing their hearts and mind to hear from Him.

Assign reading chapter 12 in preparation for next week's study. If you think it would work better for your group, you can also read the chapter in the study.

Be creative and customize what works best for your group of women.

Chapter 12: STEWARDSHIP

DISCUSSION STARTER. After prayer and worship, review what they learned as they studied last week's session four and practice committing to their 30 minutes every day. Encourage women to discuss what they experienced during the week of study and journaling.

BIBLE STUDY #12 MEMORY VERSE:
Proverbs 24:3-4 *Any enterprise is built by wise planning, becomes strong through common sense, and profits wonderfully by keeping abreast of the facts.*

WATCH SESSION 12 VIDEO at www.GodsAmazingPlans.com

GROUP DISCUSSIONS. Refer to page 212 and review group discussion questions. You can break into smaller groups for discussion to encourage deeper sharing. Have each of them answer the questions and share for encouragement.

HOMEWORK. Encourage them to take time for the Homework on page 213 and to make the weekly commitment so they can spend time daily in the presence of their Father. Start today with daily prayer, worship, and journaling. Encourage them to read it daily and pray over what they have written and ask God to start preparing their hearts and mind to hear from Him.

After they have written their testimony, share them with one another next week as you celebrate and pray for each other to continue with their journey.

Send Tamara your testimony and review so she can praise God for His work in them and continue to pray for their growth and development.

Be creative and customize what works best for your group of women.

CELEBRATION

DISCUSSION STARTER. After prayer and worship, review what they learned as they studied last week's lesson plan and congratulate them on their hard work and commitment to their 30 minutes every day. Encourage women to discuss what they experienced during the week of study and journaling.

WATCH CELEBRATION VIDEO at
www.GodsAmazingPlans.com

After they have written their testimony, share them with one another next week as you celebrate and pray for each other to continue with their journey.

WRITE TESTIMONIES AND SHARE WITH AMAZING LIFE MINISTRIES AND YOUR CIRCLES OF INFLUENCE.
SEND TESTIMONIES TO WWW.GODSAMAZINGPLANS.COM

Send Tamara your testimony and review so she can praise God for His work in them and continue to pray for their growth and development.

CELEBRATE what God has done through this study and these beautiful Godly women. Cheer each other on and pray for one another.

www.GodsAmazingPlans.com

SPECIAL DEDICATION AND ACKNOWLEDGMENT

Special dedication to **Denise Valdez**, my dear friend, best friend, traveling buddy, game night buddy, ready to go and do anything buddy, my greatest cheerleader, and support of all that God has done in my life. This book is dedicated in memory of you, your beautiful life, and the Godly woman you lived out so well. So many of the Godly characteristics in this book you displayed and embraced throughout your 61 years of life. I am certain that God, your Father, was so well pleased with your life on Earth, and when you met Him, He said "Well done good and faithful child." You will always be my ride-or-die girl and I will never forget you and the amazing time we had together on Earth. I cannot wait to see you again in Heaven and give you a great big kiss and hug!

Denise was an Amazing Life Ministries friend, volunteer, and supporter. She traveled with Tamara Doss often and assisted in countless ways from hospitality, book signings, community events, vendor shows, cooking, decorating, speaking engagements, conferences, prayer, teaching, and planning.

Denise was an invaluable part of the Authors Retreat when this book was created and written and oversaw "Hospitality," she shopped, prepared, decorated, cooked, and served the beautiful women in this book with humility and grace. Your contribution Denise was huge and always made everything better, not just your gifts, but your prayers and heart for all you served.

We also lost her amazing husband and best friend of 47 years only 14 days after Denise departed this Earth. Shout out to you Mondo Valdez! We love you so much and are grateful for you loving and supporting my girl Denise so well. Thank you for always letting her go away and hang out with me so we could enjoy the marvelous wonders of this life. You both will be missed!

SECOND DEDICATION AND ACKNOWLEDGEMENT

We also lost the husbands of two contributing authors, Blanca Cisneros, and Lori Bryant, since the Authors Retreat in June 2019 and so I dedicate this book also to Robert Cisneros and Bob Bryant, two great men of God who loved their families and wives well. I am so thankful for your support and love for two of my wonderful friends and Authors in this book. We also lost a husband before the retreat and would like to acknowledge Jason Guerrero for his amazing life and love with contributing Author and my friend, Cathy Guerrero.

AMAZING LIFE MINISTRIES TEAM RECOGNITION

Special thanks to the greatest team who brought their "A" game to serve and pray for these women authors and God's glory to shine through this project. The Authors were amazed at your welcoming spirit, and love and they felt like royalty! The King was in the house and so were His royal daughters. I am so grateful for each of you in my life and for walking beside me with God's dreams for my life.

Denise Valdez, Tamara Doss, Marlene Weyhgandt, and Sandy Cushing

www.GodsAmazingPlans.com

Made in the USA
Las Vegas, NV
21 January 2025